Clues2Use

Landlubbers on the Jesus Quest

eight sessions for a children's club

© Jean Elliott 2005
First published 2005

ISBN 1 84427 113 7

Scripture Union, 207–209 Queensway, Bletchley, Milton Keynes, MK2 2EB, United Kingdom
Email: info@scriptureunion.org.uk
Website: www.scriptureunion.org.uk

Scripture Union Australia, Locked Bag 2, Central Coast Business Centre, NSW 2252, Australia
Website: www.scriptureunion.org.au

Scripture Union USA, PO Box 987, Valley Forge, PA 19482, USA
Website: www.scriptureunion.org

Scripture quotations are from the Contemporary English Version © American Bible Society 1991, 1992, 1995. Used by permission/Anglicisations © British and Foreign Bible Society 1997.

British Library Cataloguing-in-Publication Data.
A catalogue record of this book is available from the British Library.

Printed and bound in Malta by Interprint.
Cover illustration by Si Smith.
Cover and internal template design by Kevin Wade of kwgraphicdesign.

With special thanks to the Wednesday Hothouse children:
Adam, Ashley, Ben, Caitlyn, Connor, Daniel, Dellyne, Elycia, Jade, Jodie B, Jodie H, Jamarl, Jack, Jez, Joe, Josh, Konna, Kevin, Laura S, Laura T, Leighanne, Liam, Luke H, Luke J, Luke S, Matthew, Paige, Shannon, Sasha, Shyan, Shantice, Stacey, Skye and Tom and the team, Margaret, Maxine and Pat.

Clues2Use makes use of *The Jesus Quest*, the JESUS film for children. This has been done in cooperation with Agapé. See page 62 for more details.

Clues2Use is an eye level club programme, part of *eye level*, Scripture Union's project to catch up with children and young people who have yet to catch sight of Jesus.

Scripture Union is an international Christian charity working with churches in more than 130 countries, providing resources to bring the good news of Jesus Christ to children, young people and families and to encourage them to develop spiritually through the Bible and prayer.

As well as our network of volunteers, staff and associates who run holidays, church-based events and school Christian groups, we produce a wide range of publications and support those who use our resources through training programmes.

Starting out

How to use Clues2Use

⊕ Introducing Clues2Use

Clues2Use has been designed to be used on its own or as a follow-up to the *Landlubbers* holiday club programme (SU 2004). The pirate theme of *Landlubbers* continues, but the storyline is completely new and does not depend on leaders or children being familiar with *Landlubbers*. (The children at the Hothouse club who trialled the material had not been part of *Landlubbers*, since it had not been published when the trial took place.)

The names Captain Yo-ho and Captain Heave-ho will be familiar to users of *Landlubbers* as will the *Landlubbers* song and references to the book of Philippians. *Clues2Use* will work with or without the song and references to Philippians, but for those following up *Landlubbers*, the song will provide continuity and children may respond well to bringing along their *Landlubbers Logbooks* and encountering familiar verses from Philippians as they arise. The 'Golden nugget' verses which run throughout *Clues2Use* are from Philippians 2:6–9. Each 'Tuned-in' prayer time also ends with a verse from Philippians.

Each session of *Clues2Use* contains a story about pirate captains Yo-ho and Heave-ho who have left the tropical island of *Landlubbers* and have arrived on the mainland. They follow clues which help them find out more about Jesus and the difference he can make to their lives. Each week's clue takes them to a real-life venue most of the children will be familiar with, eg the swimming pool, the supermarket, the park. What happens to the pirates there relates in some way to what happens in The Jesus Quest film, an episode of which is watched during each session.

The *Clues2Use* song has been written specifically for the programme. It is in the same style as the *Landlubbers* song. The *Clues2Use* theme song is available on the *Light for Everyone 2* CD, priced £14.99 (SU, 1 84427 169 2). The *Landlubbers* theme song is available on the *Light for Everyone* CD, priced £9.99 (SU, 1 84427 080 7). Both CDs contain non-confessional songs, ideal for use if you have children in your group who have no experience of Christianity.

⊕ Aims of Clues2Use

The pirates gradually realise that Jesus understands the situations they are in and he is right there with them. They also realise that these situations are helping them get to know Jesus better and understand more about him. This is what we want the children to discover, that Jesus can be found in every situation, that he is with us all the time and that he longs for us to become his friend.

The activities make very few assumptions about children's previous knowledge of the Bible or experience of a Christian community. There is plenty of scope for relationship building – with each other and God. At the heart of *Clues2Use* is the intention that children have fun as they build relationships with other children and adult leaders. In this context, leaders can naturally share Jesus and what he means to them. Over the weeks, trust will grow, as will the questions children ask and the answers they find. Our hope is that the Holy Spirit will be at work in the life of each child who attends, whether this is the first time they have been part of anything Christian or they are already part of a church community.

⊕ The Jesus Quest film

This film is a development of the world-renowned JESUS film which has been reshaped to make it more appropriate for children. Scripture Union has cooperated with Agapé to ensure the film is presented in a DVD format which works with the *Clues2Use* programme. The film has been broken up into nine chapters: one for each of the eight sessions in the *Clues2Use* programme, plus a closing chapter that explains how a child can start to follow Jesus. It is recommended that children and parents watch the video together in an introductory session as a way of beginning the programme, but also because the film carries a PG certificate. (See page 29 for details of running an introductory session.) The DVD is available in a pack with this book from Christian bookshops or from SU Mail Order (0845 07 06 006) or from Agapé (see page 62 for details).

You might also wish to offer each child a copy of the DVD to take home at the end of the club.

The Jesus Quest film follows the life of Jesus from birth to resurrection and features a group of children and their response to Jesus. Each episode covers several events in Jesus' life, so a key event has been chosen for each session (although other events are also referred to and form a focus for some activities). You will need to choose which is best for your group of children.

> If you do not have a DVD player, you can show *The Jesus Quest* on video. However, since the video is not broken into episodes, you will have to ensure you are in the right place on the tape each time. The video is available from Agapé – see page 62.

How the programme works

Each session is divided into three parts; *Give us a clue*, *On the Jesus Quest* and *In the treasure chest*. Choose some or all of the activities on offer in each part, but be sure to watch The Jesus Quest episode for the session and tell the Captains' story. One key activity is identified if you have limited time or want to focus upon one strand of the story of Jesus, marked with ⊕. The times in brackets for each activity indicate how long to allow, but do recognise the unique nature of your group which means that the timings are not one hundred per cent applicable. Be aware of the attention span of your children, their backgrounds and past experience of being part of a church community.

Activities will work with large or small groups but those which are especially appropriate for older children are marked with ⊙. Those that are particularly suitable for small groups are marked with ⊕.

Part 1: Give us a clue

This is the time to welcome the children and build relationships, as well as introduce the theme and prepare the children to learn. These activities involve movement, games, action and refreshments. Vary this section according to the mood of the children, your venue, the number of helpers and the time available. Make sure that this section does not go on so long that time for the other two sections is squeezed out.

If your group is meeting straight after school, the children may need to run around and let off steam or they may just be tired out. They will certainly need refreshments. After their evening meal they will be more relaxed. On Saturday or Sunday they will be different again. You will have to assess what best introduces them to the *Clues2Use* programme.

Ideas for those first few minutes of welcome or whenever you might have a bit of extra time are on page 14. Whatever you do, make sure the group feels properly welcomed and comfortable.

This section contains:
- The clue for the session
- A choice of games and activities introducing the theme of the session

Part 2: On the Jesus Quest

On the Jesus Quest focuses on each session's theme in detail, using the Bible passage, the DVD episode and the Captains' story.

When choosing the activities from this section, remember that some children find reading hard or just don't like it. Reading the Bible may appear hard work or boring but it doesn't have to be. After all, this is God's unique Word to us. Children can listen to it being read, they can act it out, draw it, memorise it, set it to music, pick out key words and so on. Bible reading is deliberately central to this programme. That is why the key Bible passages are included (see pages 15–18) so that you can put them on an OHP acetate or reproduce them in some way. The Bible will be part of a child's life long after you have left and the club has ended, so be imaginative in how you use it! Your enthusiasm for God's Word will be infectious.

All the Bible passages come from Luke's Gospel. The Bible verses have been reproduced from the Contemporary English Version and used with permission. This version is especially good for reading out loud. But whatever version of the Bible you use, make sure it is child-friendly and doesn't look old or out of date.

This section contains:
- The *Landlubbers* or *Clues2Use* song
- The Captains' story
- An episode of *The Jesus Quest* film
- The clue for the next session
- This session's key Bible passage (following on from the film) and how to explore it

• Alternative Bible passages to use if you think one of these better suits your group.

The Captains' stories could be photocopied and made into a book in their own right, with an exciting cover so that the story part of the programme is made as visual as possible. The episodes of the story can be found at the end of each week. Specially laid-out versions can be found on the Scripture Union website, for placing in a book.

In the trial, Jean wore a pirate's hat whenever she read the story and acquired a wonderful parrot puppet to be Nelson!

Part 3: In the treasure chest

In this section, you want to encourage the children to consolidate their learning and develop their encounter with God and his people.

Make sure you end properly and as calmly as possible. Try to say goodbye to each child personally. The children will be more likely then to remember what they have learnt and be aware of the positive relationships there have been in the club. Friendships made with other children and leaders may be the most important part of *Clues2Use*.

This section contains:
• Ideas for refreshments, the Landlubbers cafe
• A choice of activities
• Tuned-in creative prayer ideas

The Hothouse

Throughout *Clues2Use* you will find references to 'the Hothouse'. This is because the Hothouse children helped to pilot the material. The Hothouse is a children's and families' venue run by the churches in Aldridge, West Midlands. It's 'the place where children, young people and their families can meet, belong and discover the love of Jesus'. This converted shop, in the middle of a small parade of shops which serve an estate,is a bright, lively place and the children who come are bright and lively too! Jean Elliott, the author, who piloted the material writes: I'm very grateful to them and to the rest of the Hothouse team for sharing the *Clues2Use* journey with me.

Refreshments

Food always goes down well at the Hothouse. Eating together provides a good opportunity for chatting with children and building good relationships, so try to find time for the Landlubbers cafe. You may need to have it at the start of the programme or later. Remember to check for food allergies among the children and let parents/carers know in advance if you are planning to have something more substantial like fish and chips! If you are going to do a fair amount of food preparation, you will need to have a team member who has a basic food hygiene qualification.

Preparation

Be as well prepared as you can for each session by reading the aims, key Bible passage and 'Notes for you' section. Familiarise yourself with *The Jesus Quest* episode and the Captains' story, and choose a range of activities that are most suitable for your group. Use the checklist to make sure you have all you need for the session. If possible, plan the programme with the rest of the team so that different people can be responsible for preparing individual activities. Even if this is not possible, meet with your team before each session starts so that everyone is familiar with the aims and content, and can pray for the children and the session. There are opportunities for lots of fun and activity in *Clues2Use* and there is plenty of choice. However, it is vitally important that the Bible focus is an integral part of what you do. The overall aim of *Clues2Use* is for the children to have a great time finding out about who Jesus is, why he came, how he's interested in them and wants to meet them and be their friend, making a difference in their lives, right where they are.

Enjoy developing *Clues2Use* in your own way. Don't worry if you don't always complete all you have planned. Sometimes children are more responsive than at other times. Sometimes an activity will go so well that you want to repeat it. However, keep to the basic structure so that the children will feel secure and there is an overall balance.

Above all, have a great time getting to know Jesus better and sharing him with the children as you get to know them and hopefully some of their families too. 'I pray that God will take care of all your needs with the wonderful blessings that come from Christ Jesus!' Philippians 4:19.

Jean Elliott

Getting to know you

🕐 Building relationships

The children you'll meet at *Clues2Use* live in a fast-moving, sophisticated, technology-orientated world, dominated by screens. There is so much 'stuff' demanding their attention. Rather than trying to compete with that sort of environment, offer them what they are often missing elsewhere – real communication. Concentrate on the unique opportunity you have to build relationships, listen to them, talk with them, and give them time as you show them God's love in action. That way they will get to know you, each other and Jesus on their *Clues2Use* adventure, and have a great time too!

🕐 Top tips for sharing Jesus with children

- **Build strong friendships.** Be genuinely interested in their lives, homes, interests, what happens at school. These friendships will be bridges across which Jesus can walk! Ensure that these children know that you appreciate and respect them.
- **Be informed** about what is happening at school and home – it's useful to be in the know about sports days, class excursions or family events, and these may explain why the children are excited or tired, or both!
- **Get to know the children's families:** understand their home lives, and help their parents (or whoever is responsible for their care) know what they are learning. Children can never be divorced from their home backgrounds. Avoid talking about Mum *and* Dad. It's best to refer to Mum *or* Dad or even, 'whoever looks after you at home'.
- **Remember birthdays,** or ask someone else to take on the responsibility of noting dates and preparing cards, perhaps for the other children to sign.
- **Do as you say!** The children need to see you model what you teach them. Your friendship with Jesus matters. How else will the children see what it means in practice to be in a relationship with him?
- **Encourage everyone to join in** – adults and children alike. Create a 'we're in this together' feel to the sessions, rather than 'them and us' – avoid organising activities that adults stand and watch. Relax, have fun and learn with the children – '…aim to give children the best hour of their week!' (Dave Connelly, Frontline Church)
- **Mind your language!** Avoid jargon words (eg sin, grace or churchy words) and explain what you mean by things like prayer.
- **Use illustrations from everyday life** to explain concepts. Jesus taught complex truths in simple ways (eg you can't see wind, but you can see the effects that it has; it's the same with the Holy Spirit). You will need to think about this before the club begins.
- **Grow confidence with the Bible** and explain how to read it. Why don't we often start at page 1? How do we use the contents page? (Younger children find this very hard.) What are the differences between chapters and verses, or the Old and New Testaments? How do you explain that the Bible is one big story – God's story – in different bits? Find out more about the Bible in *The Story of the Book* (see the bottom of the page).
- **Talk about Jesus**, rather than God, where possible. The Gospels give us clear pictures of what he is like and these are far easier to grasp than the idea of God being 'up there' but invisible. Children have some very woolly ideas about God, but there is less room for manoeuvre when it comes to Jesus!
- **Apply the Bible teaching appropriately.** 'If Jesus arrived in your town, like he arrived in Jerusalem, what do you think he would say and do? How do you think people would welcome him?' Help the children see that Jesus is alive today (even though we can't see him) and is relevant to their lives.
- **Allow children to make responses** that are appropriate for them, their understanding and their backgrounds. Don't rush straight in with, 'Do you want to follow Jesus?' That should be a decision that lasts for life, and they need to recognise what it entails. For many children, there are a number of commitments as their understanding grows.
- **Have fun together!** The children need to catch something of the 'life in all its fullness' that Jesus spoke about.

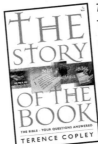

The Story of the Book
Terence Copley
£8.99 1 84427 131 5

Find out more about the Bible: Who wrote it? How was it put together? What is its future? These difficult questions and more are answered in a down-to-earth style in this 'unstuffy' book about God's Word.

Working with small groups

⊕ Practicalities

- Children are all different. Respect their differences.
- Make sure any child with a special need is catered for.
- Make sure children know they can come to you with any questions.
- Make sure that children are comfortable. Cold, hard floors do not encourage positive discussion. Cushions, mats or comfortable chairs can make all the difference. Sometimes, everyone lying on their tummies in a star shape can create a fantastic atmosphere – their teacher at school is unlikely to do this.
- Keep good eye contact with every child.
- In the group, watch out for children who are on the edge.
- Don't talk down to children – talk with them. This means getting to their level, physically and verbally.
- Don't always rush to fill silences while children are thinking of responses.
- Validate all responses, either by a further question or ask others what they think, especially if you don't agree with the initial comment or answer.
- If lots of children want to talk, pass an object round – only the child holding the object can speak.
- Encourage children to listen to each other (something they might find quite difficult).
- Be prepared to admit that you don't know the answer to a question, but say that you'll find out the answer, if appropriate.

⊕ Asking questions

There are plenty of opportunities in *Clues2Use* for asking the children questions about the Bible passage and encouraging their thinking about Jesus. A discussion is most appropriate when the children are in small groups as they don't need to wait as long for an opportunity to speak.

Ever thought about the kinds of questions you ask people? The same question can be asked in many different ways, and force the person being asked the question to give certain kinds of answers.

?? Rhetorical

If you ask, 'Isn't it great to have ice cream?', it is a rhetorical question, implying the expected answer. It brings out the right answer for the benefit of others.

?? Closed

If you ask, 'Do you like coming to *Clues2Use*?', it is a closed question, mainly allowing for 'Yes' or 'No'. It encourages contributions and assesses what the children think.

?? Factual

If you ask, 'What animal did Jesus ride into Jerusalem on?', it is a factual question, requiring basic information. It encourages contributions and establishes the facts.

?? Open

If you ask, 'Why did Jesus choose a donkey to ride on when he arrived in Jerusalem?', it is an open question, allowing broad expression. It encourages discussion and indicates what the children think.

?? Experience

If you ask, 'How would you feel if you were in the crowd when Jesus arrived?', it is an experience question, for sharing views or feelings. It encourages discussion and helps children to apply the teaching personally.

?? Leading

If you ask, 'What have you learnt at *Clues2Use*, Anna?', it is a leading question aimed at getting a specific answer from someone. It indicates learning and understanding and encourages contributions.

Think about when you might use these types of questions in your group. Go through each question with your team and decide when it is appropriate and when it is inappropriate to use certain kinds of questions.

Helping children respond

🔄 Being Jesus' friend

Clues2Use introduces children to people from the Gospels who were on the Jesus Quest (as well as our fictional pirates!). They'll also meet people in the 21st century who know and love Jesus. This may prompt children to want to be friends with Jesus for themselves. Be ready to help them.

- They rarely need long explanations, just simple answers to questions.
- Talk to them in a place where you can be seen by others.
- Never put pressure on children to respond in a particular way, just help them take one step closer to Jesus when they are ready. We don't want them to respond just to please us!
- Remember, for many children there are a number of commitments as their understanding grows.
- Many children just need a bit of help to say what they want to say to God. Here is a suggested prayer they could use to make a commitment to Jesus:

> Jesus, I want to be your friend.
> Thank you that you love me.
> Thank you for living in the world and dying on a cross for me.
> I'm sorry for all the wrong things I have done.
> Please forgive me and let me be your friend.
> Please let the Holy Spirit help me be like you.
> Amen

Reassure them that God hears us when we talk with him, and has promised to forgive us and help us be his friends.

The ninth chapter of *The Jesus Quest* DVD explains how a child can become a follower of Jesus. You may not wish to use this with your group since you have built a relationship with the children and can explain personally what it means to follow Jesus. However, it may help focus your discussion.

🔄 What next?

Children need help to stick with Jesus, especially if their parents don't believe.

- Assure them that God wants them to talk with him, whatever they want to say. Give them some prayer ideas.
- Encourage them to keep coming to Christian activities, not necessarily on Sundays – their church might have to be the midweek club or a school lunch-time club.
- Reading the Bible will be easier with something like *Snapshots* – but you need to support them if they are to keep it up.
- Keep praying and maintain your relationship with them wherever possible.

🔄 Some booklets that may help

From Scripture Union

Friends with Jesus
A booklet explaining what it means to make a commitment to follow Jesus for under-8s.
Single copy £0.99 1 84427 141 2
Pack of 20 £15.00 1 84427 144 7

Me+Jesus
A booklet explaining what it means to make a commitment to follow Jesus for 8 to 10s.
Single copy £0.99 1 84427 142 0
Pack of 20 £15.00 1 84427 145 5

Jesus=friendship forever
A booklet explaining what it means to make a commitment to follow Jesus for 10 to 12s.
Single copy £0.99 1 84427 143 9
Pack of 20 £15.00 1 84427 146 3

What Jesus did
D Abrahall
A book exploring Jesus, ideal for those with special needs.
Single copy £2.00
1 84427 005 X
Pack of 5 with teachers' guide
£8.00 1 84427 006 8

Snapshots
Bible reading for 8- to 10-year-olds.
Single copy £2.50
Annual subscription (UK) £9.00
Packs of 6 £12.50
4-week challenge £.0.99 1 84427 086 6

For a simple commitment card, visit the eye level website: www.scriptureunion.org.uk/eyelevel

Prices are correct at the time of going to press.

Sharing your faith

So many people put their trust in Jesus because they have heard how important he is to someone else. You have a great opportunity to share with the children what Jesus means to different people, and also to show by the way you live your own life that Jesus really is alive! Here are some pointers to bear in mind when you're talking with children about what Jesus means to you:

- Make sure you don't use Christian jargon or concepts that just don't make sense – 'Inviting Jesus into your heart' might suggest to some children that Jesus is only welcome in a bit of them. The idea of a person you can't see living inside your body can be a bit spooky!
- Remember you are talking to children whose experience of life is not as broad as an adult's, so their uncertainties and questions are different. Address their issues by referring to experiences which are relevant to them. This is not necessarily just what it was like for you when you were a child! But, for example, the emotions you experienced when you recently changed job may be very similar to those of a child changing school. God was with you then, so can be with a child.
- Speak about Jesus as someone you know and are enthusiastic about.
- Make reference to what the Bible says in a way that makes a child want to read the Bible for themselves – sound enthusiastic about what God has said to us. Hold the Bible with respect and read with interest. Tell a Bible story briefly to explain a point.
- Be brief and speak with simple sentences, using appropriate language.
- Be honest, talking about the good and the bad times. God doesn't always give answers, or the answers we want.
- It is important to talk about what Jesus means to us now and not when we first came to know him dozens of years ago.

If you are involved in up-front presentation, there are some other points to consider:
- An interview process is less intense, and invites the children to engage with what the interviewee is saying.
- Include questions or information about subjects such as favourite colours, food, team, job, hopes, worst moments, as well as favourite Bible character or story. Think what a child is curious about. 'Normal' information communicates that being a Christian is all about Jesus being with us all the time, being normal!
- Not everyone's experience will be appropriate, however dramatic it might be! Long and complicated stories will lose children. A wide age range will also determine what is suitable.
- Use someone's story that is relevant to the theme of the day.
- Choose a variety of people with different experiences to share what Jesus means to them over the week.
- It would be worth the team hearing what is going to be said in advance, if someone's experience is going to raise questions that may be a challenge to answer.

Whether you're speaking in front of the whole club, or one child, you should be ready to tell your story. Think beforehand about what you are going to say, just as you would practise music or drama. It isn't a speech but there is no excuse for rambling.

Practical considerations

It is important to think about child protection when running your club. If your midweek club has already been in existence for some time, you have probably made all the necessary arrangements. However, if you are just starting up a midweek club, there is child protection advice on the Scripture Union website. For advice specific to running a holiday club, see the child protection section in *Landlubbers*.

What to do after Clues2Use

❶ Step one – time to think

Hopefully, *Clues2Use* has made you think about how you run activities and reach out to children in your community. Before the end of the *Clues2Use* series, plan a review with anyone who helped. Be as honest as you can and dream dreams!

- What did the children enjoy about *Clues2Use*?
- What was different compared to your previous activities for children?
- Were there more small-group activities? How did they work?
- Was there more Bible input than before?
- What worked really well or didn't work?
- What did the leaders enjoy?
- What did you discover about each other's gifts for working with children? Was there an unknown storyteller or someone especially good at welcoming children?

Write down the most important answers. Talk about what you should do next.

Have you thought about offering each child their very own copy of *The Jesus Quest* DVD? You could either offer these to the children at the end of the programme or go to visit each child in their home – an opportunity to get to know the families a bit better. The DVDs are available from Agapé. For details, turn to page 62.

❷ Step two – moving on

Don't be afraid to develop what you provide for children. If *Clues2Use* encouraged you to run a midweek or Saturday club for the first time and it worked, plan to carry on. You may need extra help, especially if some people can't commit themselves weekly. Perhaps you could do another eight-week club next term or maybe a monthly Saturday/Sunday special, using another Scripture Union programme.

Discuss how you might contact new children. What are your links with the local school(s) or neighbourhood groups? Could you publicise your group through the local paper or library? How could the children who already come be encouraged to bring their friends? Just how many more children can you cope with?

❸ Step three – building on Clues2Use

One of the aims of *Clues2Use* is to bring children who don't usually have much contact with a Christian community into a Christian activity. If this worked for you, build on the final *Clues2Use* session and get to know the children's families by running a parents' special event. Family games work well, either games to play as families or everyone all together. Any family activity that offers food will be popular! Alternatively, some churches have explored parenting groups. In one place, a church football team has developed from fathers of children who started coming to a church children's club. Be imaginative and find out what other churches have done in your area. Maybe you could do something together.

Whatever you do, it is good to maintain contact with children, to sustain and grow your relationships. You may wish to visit the children. If you do so, contact the parents to make sure they are happy for you to come and to arrange a time for your visit. Visiting the children also enables you to have contact with their parents.

✦ Other programmes

Streetwise and *Awesome!*, eight-session programmes similar in aim and design to *Clues2Use*, are already available. *Streetwise*, with an accompanying DVD (based on the *Luke Street* video), introduces children to the inhabitants of various houses Jesus visited, using Luke's Gospel. *Awesome!* and its accompanying DVD (based on the *Signposts* video) find signs to who Jesus is in the Gospel of John.

Look out for *Pyramid Rock*, a five-day holiday club programme following the story of Joseph, using Genesis as its main Bible text. Published in December 2005, *Pyramid Rock* is followed in 2006 by *Rocky Road*, a follow-up midweek programme based on the life of Moses.

Extra activities

The first and last few minutes of a club can be the most important! Your first conversation with a child helps to settle them, for them to be open to God. You represent Jesus: your welcome is his welcome. The end of the club may be what they remember best, so make the most of the time.

A few guidelines

- Choose the right opening question for the right day: if it's the weekend, keep school conversation to a minimum.
- Be led by the child. Don't probe where they don't want to talk.
- Allow a conversation to develop rather than just asking questions.
- Help others join in as they join the group.
- Tell the children about your day, to build friendships and make it less like a grilling.

Questions about school

What was the best thing that happened? Did anything funny happen? What did you have for dinner? What's the food like at your school?

General questions

What have you seen on television/read/done recently? What are you doing this weekend? How's your football team doing? Tell me about your family/what you do in your spare time.

Ideas to end the club

A routine pattern to the end may be useful.

In groups

- Chat about what they will do at home/later/during the week.
- A quick recap of the Bible teaching to help them remember/apply it.
- Pray for the week ahead.

Together

- Recap the Bible teaching and allow a moment to think about it again.
- Sit around a candle and remind them that Jesus, the light of the world, is always with us. Ask for things to pray about, or read prayers they have written during the session. (You could light the candle if you have assessed the risks and can do so safely.)
- Sing the *Landlubbers* and/or *Clues2Use* song.

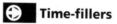 Time-fillers

1 Turn everyone's name round and enjoy the different sounds! (Nhoj Htims, Enna Senoj)

2 I Spy. For very young children play 'I spy with my colour eye', with objects of a certain colour.

3 Who can… wiggle their ears, touch their nose with their tongue, recite the alphabet backwards, wiggle their eyebrows and so on.

4 Dice games: have ready-made cards with questions to be answered when the numbers are rolled.
For example:
Favourites: 1 – food; 2 – pop group; 3 – team; 4 – TV programme; 5 – story; 6 – colour.
Home: 1 – family; 2 – rooms; 3 – pets; 4 – food; 5 – outside the house; 6 – favourite room.
Favourite food: 1 – sandwich; 2 – drink; 3 – breakfast; 4 – biscuits; 5 – snack; 6 – worst food.

5 Simon says, but with a *Clues2Use* flavour: 'Captain Yo-ho says, "Climb the rigging".'

6 'I went to the park (supermarket, football match) and I saw…' Each person recites the growing list and adds an item.

7 Mime things you do at home – others must guess, eg watching TV, turning on a tap.

8 Challenge the group to make a human sculpture of household objects, eg a chair, knife and fork, clock, bathroom.

If the children turn up in dribs and drabs, you may want to have a general activity that they can join in as they arrive. Or you might want to have an ongoing activity, which the children can do as a group craft during *In the treasure chest*.

Key Bible passages

These Bible verses for *Clues2Use* are taken from the Contemporary English Version and used with permission.

Pages 15 to 27 are photocopiable. You may photocopy any of these pages for use in your *Clues2Use* programme.

 Session 1

Luke 2:1–14

About that time Emperor Augustus gave orders for the names of all the people to be listed in record books. These first records were made when Quirinius was governor of Syria.

Everyone had to go to their own home town to be listed. So Joseph had to leave Nazareth in Galilee and go to Bethlehem in Judea. Long ago Bethlehem had been King David's home town, and Joseph went there because he was from David's family.

Mary was engaged to Joseph and travelled with him to Bethlehem. She was soon going to have a baby, and while they were there, she gave birth to her firstborn son. She dressed him in baby clothes and laid him on a bed of hay, because there was no room for them in the inn.

That night in the fields near Bethlehem some shepherds were guarding their sheep. All at once an angel came down to them from the Lord, and the brightness of the Lord's glory flashed around them. The shepherds were frightened. But the angel said, "Don't be afraid! I have good news for you, which will make everyone happy. This very day in King David's home town a Saviour was born for you. He is Christ the Lord. You will know who he is, because you will find him dressed in baby clothes and lying on a bed of hay."

Suddenly many other angels came down from heaven and joined in praising God. They said:

"Praise God in heaven!
Peace on earth to everyone
who pleases God."

 Session 2

Luke 5:1–11

Jesus was standing on the shore of Lake Gennesaret, teaching the people as they crowded around him to hear God's message. Near the shore he saw two boats left there by some fishermen who had gone to wash their nets. Jesus got into the boat that belonged to Simon and asked him to row it out a little way from the shore. Then Jesus sat down in the boat to teach the crowd.

When Jesus had finished speaking, he told Simon, "Row the boat out into the deep water and let your nets down to catch some fish."

"Master," Simon answered, "we have worked hard all night long and have not caught a thing. But if you tell me to, I will let the nets down." They did it and caught so many fish that their nets began ripping apart. Then they signalled for their partners in the other boat to come and help them. The men came, and together they filled the two boats so full that they both began to sink.

When Simon Peter saw this happen, he knelt down in front of Jesus and said, "Lord, don't come near me! I am a sinner." Peter and everyone with him were completely surprised at all the fish they had caught. His partners James and John, the sons of Zebedee, were surprised too.

Jesus told Simon, "Don't be afraid! From now on you will bring in people instead of fish." The men pulled their boats up on the shore. Then they left everything and went with Jesus.

Luke 5:27–32

Later, Jesus went out and saw a tax collector named Levi sitting at the place for paying taxes. Jesus said to him, "Come with me." Levi left everything and went with Jesus.

In his home Levi gave a big dinner for Jesus. Many tax collectors and other guests were also there.

The Pharisees and some of their teachers of the Law of Moses grumbled to Jesus' disciples, "Why do you eat and drink with those tax collectors and other sinners?"

Jesus answered, "Healthy people don't need a doctor, but sick people do. I didn't come to invite good people to turn to God. I came to invite sinners."

Session 3

Luke 8:4–8

When a large crowd from several towns had gathered around Jesus, he told them this story:

A farmer went out to scatter seed in a field. While the farmer was doing it, some of the seeds fell along the road and were stepped on or eaten by birds. Other seeds fell on rocky ground and started growing. But the plants did not have enough water and soon dried up.Some other seeds fell where thorn bushes grew up and choked the plants. The rest of the seeds fell on good ground where they grew and produced a hundred times as many seeds.

When Jesus had finished speaking, he said, "If you have ears, pay attention!"

Session 4

Luke 9:10–17

The apostles came back and told Jesus everything they had done. He then took them with him to the village of Bethsaida, where they could be alone. But a lot of people found out about this and followed him. Jesus welcomed them. He spoke to them about God's kingdom and healed everyone who was sick.

Late in the afternoon the twelve apostles came to Jesus and said, "Send the crowd to the villages and farms around here. They need to find a place to stay and something to eat. There is nothing in this place. It is like a desert!"

Jesus answered, "You give them something to eat."

But they replied, "We have only five small loaves of bread and two fish. If we are going to feed all these people, we will have to go and buy food." There were about five thousand men in the crowd.

Jesus said to his disciples, "Tell the people to sit in groups of fifty." They did this, and all the people sat down. Jesus took the five loaves and the two fish. He looked up towards heaven and blessed the food. Then he broke the bread and fish and handed them to his disciples to give to the people.

Everyone ate all they wanted. What was left over filled twelve baskets.

Session 5

Luke 19:28–38

When Jesus had finished saying all this, he went on towards Jerusalem. As he was getting near Bethphage and Bethany on the Mount of Olives, he sent two of his disciples on ahead. He told them, "Go into the next village, where you will find a young donkey that has never been ridden. Untie the donkey and bring it here. If anyone asks why you are doing that, just say, 'The Lord needs it.'"

They went off and found everything just as Jesus had said. While they were untying the donkey, its owners asked, "Why are you doing that?"

They answered, "The Lord needs it."

Then they led the donkey to Jesus. They put some of their clothes on its back and helped Jesus get on. And as he rode along, the people spread clothes on the road in front of him. When Jesus was setting off down the Mount of Olives, his large crowd of disciples were happy and praised God because of all the miracles they had seen.

They shouted,

"Blessed is the king who comes
    in the name of the Lord!
Peace in heaven
    and glory to God."

Session 6

Luke 22:39–53

Jesus went out to the Mount of Olives, as he often did, and his disciples went with him. When they got there, he told them, "Pray that you won't be tested."

Jesus walked on a little way before he knelt down and prayed, "Father, if you will, please don't make me suffer by making me drink from this cup. But do what you want, and not what I want."

Then an angel from heaven came to help him. Jesus was in great pain and prayed so sincerely that his sweat fell to the ground like drops of blood.

Jesus got up from praying and went over to his disciples. They were asleep and worn out from being so sad. He said to them, "Why are you asleep? Wake up and pray that you won't be tested."

While Jesus was still speaking, a crowd came up. It was led by Judas, one of the twelve apostles. He went over to Jesus and greeted him with a kiss.

Jesus asked Judas, "Are you betraying the Son of Man with a kiss?"

When Jesus' disciples saw what was about to happen, they asked, "Lord, should we attack them with a sword?" One of the disciples even struck at the high priest's servant with his sword and cut off the servant's right ear.

"Enough of that!" Jesus said. Then he touched the servant's ear and healed it.

Jesus spoke to the chief priests, the temple police, and the leaders who had come to arrest him. He said, "Why do you come out with swords and clubs and treat me like a criminal? I was with you every day in the temple, and you didn't arrest me. But this is your time, and darkness is in control."

Session 7

Luke 23:26–27

As Jesus was being led away, some soldiers grabbed hold of a man from Cyrene named Simon. He was coming in from the fields, but they put the cross on him and made him carry it behind Jesus.

A large crowd was following Jesus, and in the crowd a lot of women were crying and weeping for him.

Luke 23:32–49

Two criminals were led out to be put to death with Jesus. When the soldiers came to the place called "The Skull", they nailed Jesus to a cross. They also nailed the two criminals to crosses, one on each side of Jesus.

Jesus said, "Father, forgive these people! They don't know what they're doing."

While the crowd stood there watching Jesus, the soldiers gambled for his clothes. The leaders insulted him by saying, "He saved others. Now he should save himself, if he really is God's chosen Messiah!"

The soldiers made fun of Jesus and brought him some wine. They said, "If you are the king of the Jews, save yourself!"

Above him was a sign that said, "This is the King of the Jews."

One of the criminals hanging there also insulted Jesus by saying, "Aren't you the Messiah? Save yourself and save us!"

But the other criminal told the first one off, "Don't you fear God? Aren't you getting the same punishment as this man? We got what was coming to us, but he didn't do anything wrong." Then he said to Jesus, "Remember me when you come into power!"

Jesus replied, "I promise that today you will be with me in paradise."

Around midday the sky turned dark and stayed that way until the middle of the afternoon. The sun stopped shining, and the curtain in the temple split down the middle. Jesus shouted, "Father, I put myself in your hands!" Then he died.

When the Roman officer saw what had happened, he praised God and said, "Jesus must really have been a good man!"

A crowd had gathered to see the terrible sight. Then after they had seen it, they felt brokenhearted and went home. All Jesus' close friends and the women who had come with him from Galilee stood at a distance and watched.

Session 8

Luke 24:1–10

Very early on Sunday morning the women went to the tomb, carrying the spices that they had prepared. When they found the stone rolled away from the entrance, they went in. But they did not find the body of the Lord Jesus, and they did not know what to think.

Suddenly two men in shining white clothes stood beside them. The women were afraid and bowed to the ground. But the men said, "Why are you looking in the place of the dead for someone who is alive? Jesus isn't here! He has been raised from death. Remember that while he was still in Galilee, he told you, 'The Son of Man will be handed over to sinners who will nail him to a cross. But three days later he will rise to life.'" Then they remembered what Jesus had said.

Mary Magdalene, Joanna, Mary the mother of James, and some other women were the ones who had gone to the tomb. When they returned, they told the eleven apostles and the others what had happened.

Luke 24:36–43

While Jesus' disciples were talking about what had happened, Jesus appeared and greeted them. They were frightened and terrified because they thought they were seeing a ghost.

But Jesus said, "Why are you so frightened? Why do you doubt? Look at my hands and my feet and see who I am! Touch me and find out for yourselves. Ghosts don't have flesh and bones as you see I have."

After Jesus said this, he showed them his hands and his feet. The disciples were so glad and amazed that they could not believe it. Jesus then asked them, "Do you have something to eat?" They gave him a piece of baked fish. He took it and ate it as they watched.

How to use the clue cards on page 19

Fold an A4 sheet of card for each child in your club. Ask them to write 'Clue card' on the front, and let them decorate the front as they wish. Each session, give each child the appropriate clue and let them stick it inside. Encourage them to write the solution next to the clue. You may like to ask them to write any thoughts they have about each session on the card too.

Decorate the front

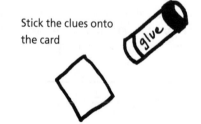

Stick the clues onto the card

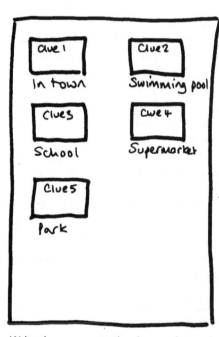

Write the answers to the clues underneath

Clue 1

Find a house – an empty one,
With broken windows, not much fun.
Still, it will be a place to rest,
Where you can start the Jesus Quest.

Clue 2

Changing rooms and lots of noise,
Lifeguards with their whistles poised.
Water sparkling blue and green,
We even have a wave machine.

Clue 3

A building where you go to learn,
Though some can't wait till end of term!
Landlubbers, do your very best
On the next part of the Jesus Quest.

Clue 4

Checkouts, music, special offers,
Rushing, dreaming mass of shoppers.
So much choice down every aisle,
Then stand and queue for half a mile!

Clue 5

A place with grass to run and play,
Its gates are open every day.
There are swings and a slide if you
want a game, but
My favourite is the climbing frame!

Clue 6

People arriving with grapes
and flowers,
Patients look forward to visiting hours.
Nurses, caring, smiling, smart,
Doctors checking someone's heart.

Clue 7

Flags and scarves, a cheer, a shout!
Now the teams are coming out.
Free kick! Corner! Mexican wave.
Will it go in? Wow! What a save!

Clue 8

Landlubbers, here's your invitation,
You're welcome at the celebration.
You've looked north and south,
east and west.
Today you'll complete the Jesus Quest!

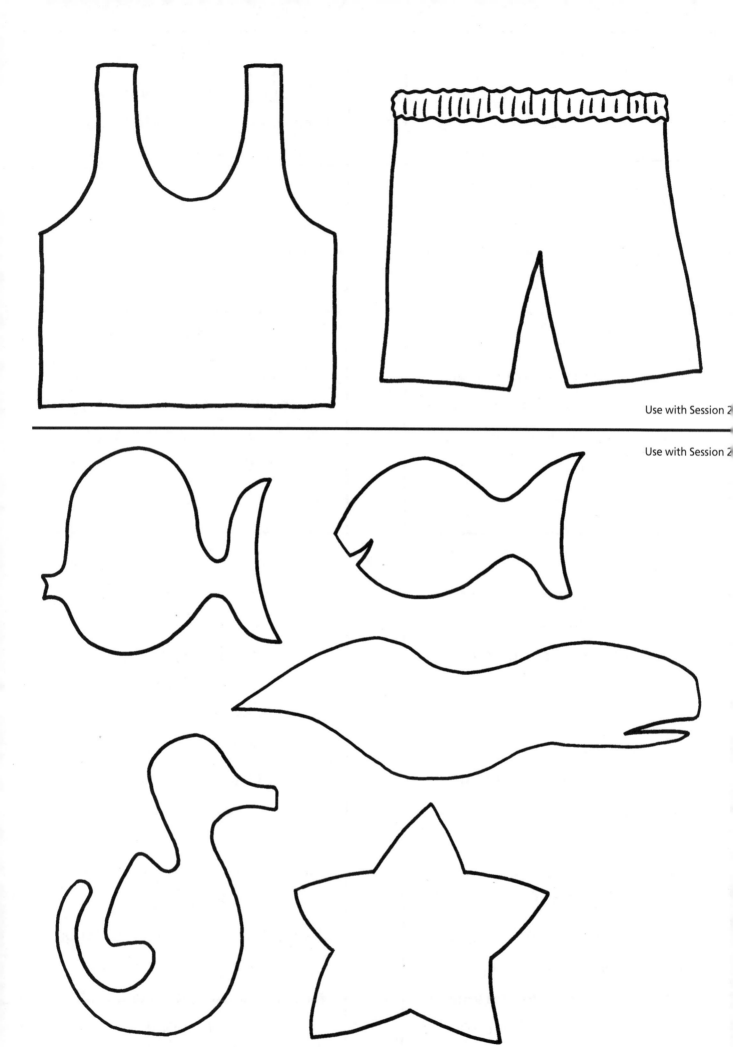

Use with Session 2

Use with Session 2

Use with Session 2

Use with Session 6

Use with Session 8

Use with Session 4

Use with Session 8

Mary	Shepherd	Anna
An angel came to visit me. He gave me astonishing news! He said I would have a special baby.	I don't have much money. I work out on the hills. Angels invited me to visit a new king in a stable!	I'm 84 years old. I spend a lot of time at the temple, praying. I was able to hold God's special baby.
Teacher of the law	**John the Baptist**	**Man at synagogue**
I know a lot of things about God, but the questions of a 12-year-old boy made me think very hard.	I baptise people who want a new start with God. To my surprise, Jesus came to be baptised with everyone else!	I was in the meeting place in Nazareth. Joseph's boy Jesus stood up to read. He amazed us by saying the words had just come true!

Use with Session 1

(Mary and the angel: Luke 1:26–33)

Jesus is coming!

(Stable and shepherds: Luke 2:8–14)

Jesus is born!

(Simeon and Anna: Luke 2:25–28,36–38)

Jesus is the one we've been waiting for!

Use with Session 4

(At the temple, age 12: Luke 2:41–49)

Jesus grows up!

(Baptism: Luke 3:2b,3,21,22)

Jesus is ready to start!

(Reading the scroll: Luke 4:16–21)

Jesus is good news!

Use with Session 1

Possible questions

To mugged person:
- Can you describe what happened to you?
- How did you feel when the priest and Levite walked straight past you?
- How did you feel when the Samaritan stopped to help you?

To priest:
- Why did you leave that poor, injured person lying by the roadside?

To Levite:
- Let me ask you the same question.

To Samaritan:
- You're from a country that once had a big argument with the injured man's country. Why did you stop and help?

To hotel manager:
- What did you think when these two people arrived at your hotel?

Clues2Use

Rocky feel

Words and music by
Ruth Wills

Je - sus teach - er,___ Je - sus lead - er,___ Je - sus sav - iour, friend and king.___ We are list - 'ning,___ we are learn - ing,___ all the good news that he brings.

1. Fol - low - ing Je - sus ev - 'ry - where,___ fol - low - ing Je - sus ev - 'ry - where,___ fol - low - ing Je - sus wher - ev - er we may be, and he's with you and

2. Fol - low - ing Je - sus ev - 'ry - where,___ fol - low - ing Je - sus ev - 'ry - where,___ fol - low - ing Je - sus wher - ev - er we may be, and he's with you and

he's with me all the time!_____ swim - ming pool, all the
he's with me at the

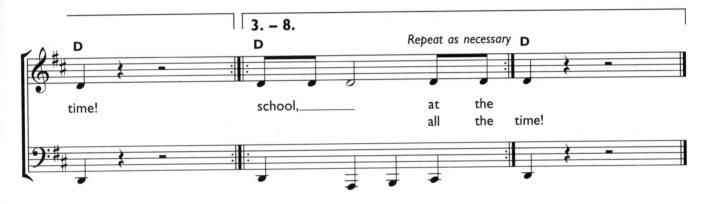

time! school,_____ at the
all the time!

Repeat as necessary

8. Following Jesus ev'rywhere,
   Following Jesus ev'rywhere,
   Following Jesus wherever we may be,
   And he's with you and he's with me
   At a party,
   At the football,
   At the hospital,
   At the park,
   At the shops,
   At school,
   At the swimming pool,
   All the time!

Chorus
Jesus teacher, Jesus leader, Jesus saviour, friend and king.
We are listening, we are learning,
All the good news that he brings.

1 Following Jesus everywhere,
Following Jesus everywhere,
Following Jesus wherever we may be,
And he's with you and he's with me all the time!

Repeat chorus

2 Following Jesus everywhere, *(x2)*
Following Jesus wherever we may be,
And he's with you and he's with me at the swimming pool,
All the time!

Repeat chorus

3 Following Jesus everywhere, *(x2)*
Following Jesus wherever we may be,
And he's with you and he's with me at school,
At the swimming pool,
All the time!

Repeat chorus

4 Following Jesus everywhere, *(x2)*
Following Jesus wherever we may be,
And he's with you and he's with me at the shops,
At school, at the swimming pool,
All the time!

Repeat chorus

Written by Ruth Wills © Scripture Union 2005

CCLI licence number: _____

Clues2Use
Landlubbers on the Jesus Quest

5 Following Jesus everywhere, *(x2)*
Following Jesus wherever we may be,
And he's with you and he's with me at the park,
At the shops, at school, at the swimming pool,
All the time!

Repeat chorus

6 Following Jesus everywhere, *(x2)*
Following Jesus wherever we may be,
And he's with you and he's with me at the hospital,
At the park, at the shops, at school, at the swimming pool,
All the time!

Repeat chorus

7 Following Jesus everywhere, *(x2)*
Following Jesus wherever we may be,
And he's with you and he's with me at the football,
At the hospital, at the park, at the shops, at school,
At the swimming pool,
All the time!

Repeat chorus

8 Following Jesus everywhere, *(x2)*
Following Jesus wherever we may be,
And he's with you and he's with me at a party,
At the football, at the hospital, at the park,
At the shops, at school, at the swimming pool,
All the time!

Written by Ruth Wills © Scripture Union 2005

CCLI licence number: _____

Landlubbers
at the cinema

⏱ The Jesus Quest premiere

What you need
- A copy of *The Jesus Quest* DVD
- Either a video projector and large screen, or a good-sized television and DVD player
- Popcorn
- Other refreshments

What you do

The *Clues2Use* programme starts with a film night, as Captains Yo-ho and Heave-ho arrive on the mainland and go to the cinema. This is a great introduction to the club, but it also serves to give a chance for you to show *The Jesus Quest* DVD to the parents of the children who will come to your club. As *The Jesus Quest* DVD carries a PG (Parental Guidance) certificate, it is a necessary requirement that all parents/guardians have an opportunity to see the film themselves. You will also be able to start relationships with parents at the beginning of the *Clues2Use* programme.

Before the session, send out invitations to children who you would like to come to your club – those who already come to a club, their friends or links through schools or a holiday club. Include pictures of pirates, parrots and other Landlubbers-style illustrations. You might like to include this extra clue on the invitations, so that the children get a feel for the club:

> Popcorn, drinks, ice cream and sweets,
> A fantastic place for us to meet,
> Watch a film on the big screen,
> It's the only place to be seen!

Set the scene by giving out popcorn and drinks as you arrive, and by blacking out the windows and setting the chairs in rows to create the impression of a cinema. Arrange for your team to be the 'cinema employees' – you may want to give out tickets as the children arrive, then check them as they enter the 'cinema' room. Use your imagination to make this a memorable and exciting experience.

Place the first clue of the Jesus Quest in one of the bags of popcorn for you or one of the other leaders to 'find' at an appropriate time during the session (decide when before the session starts). When the clue is found, read it out and get the children to try and guess what it means.

> Find a house – an empty one,
> With broken windows, not much fun.
> Still, it will be a place to rest,
> Where you can start the Jesus Quest.

🅖 *At the Hothouse we planned an interval half way through the film. We made it clear to the children that there would be an opportunity to move around and have a drink and popcorn during the interval. We asked them to stay in their seats while the film was actually on. (Everyone had a selection of sweets!) It was hard for some of them to sit for a full-length film but the arrangements worked well. They particularly enjoyed the surprise of the clue in the popcorn during the interval.* 🅖

At the end of the session, make sure that everyone knows when the next session of *Clues2Use* is happening.

🅖 *Sadly, we didn't have any parents at the Hothouse film evening, but they were happy to complete the consent forms. Later on in the series though, one parent did stay for a session and asked to borrow the film to take home, so it is well worth buying a few spare copies of the DVD to make this possible!* 🅖

Parental consent

When you send out your invitations it is important to include a consent form for parents/guardians to sign, giving permission for their children to watch *The Jesus Quest* even if they themselves do not want to come, or are unable to come, to the introductory session. You could offer to lend a copy of the DVD to any parent/guardian who would like to see it at home. You might also offer a copy of the DVD to the children at the end of the programme. For details of how to get this from Agapé see page 62.

Session 1

Luke
2:1–14

Aim To hear that Jesus was born as a baby in a way which was carefully planned by God, and that he grew up and was ready to do the special work God had for him.

Landlubbers
arrive in town

Notes for you

Jesus was born into the mess of this world in a humble animal shelter. Right from the beginning there were people who were ready to recognise who he was. Pray that the children will understand that Jesus is able to be involved with them, right where they are, and that they will begin to recognise who he is and why he is good news.

The Christmas story is one of the few Bible stories children will be familiar with, but they may have misunderstood it! This is an opportunity to check out what they already know.

The Jesus Quest episode includes: Jesus' birth, his presentation in the temple, his visit to the temple at the age of 12, the reading of the scroll in the synagogue.

The key story is the birth of Jesus.

Give us a clue

Welcome the children and give them each a clue card. Ask them to write their name on it and then give them the first clue (about the ramshackle house, see page 19) to stick on the card. Help the children read the clue so they remember where the Landlubbers will be going today. Then collect in the clue cards ready for next time.

1 Ready for the baby!
(10 minutes)

What you need

- A large sheet of paper or card for each group – in the centre of the paper there should be a picture of a baby drawn or stuck on
- Drawing materials

What you do

Divide the children into groups. Give each group their baby picture and give them a time limit in which they should draw as many things as possible around the baby that it will need when it's born (eg toys, clothes, nappies, bottle, cot, car seat, towels, bath). At the end of the time, look at the pictures together and see what each group thinks their baby will need!

This introduces the idea of a story about a baby and that God had planned Jesus' birth very carefully.

The Hothouse children enjoyed this game. All the babies had potties and one had a full Aston Villa football strip!

2 Angel art gallery
(10 minutes)

What you need

- Dark coloured background paper
- Crayons and paints (including gold, silver and white), glitter (optional!)
- Pictures of angels (optional)

Jesus – the promised one

What you do

Ask the children to think about what an angel looks like. Chat together about the ideas the children have. Look at pictures of angels, if you have them. Show the children the materials you have and ask them to create a picture of an angel. While the children are doing this, continue their discussion about angels. Enjoy looking at the results together. This helps to introduce angels – you'll encounter them later!

3 Scrap art
(10 minutes)

What you need

- A variety of boxes, tubes and cartons
- Scissors and plenty of sticky tape

What you do

Show the children the materials you have collected together and tell them you are going to do some junk modelling. Decide together whether you are going to make individual junk models or a joint one.

As you are working, talk with the children about what rubbish there is in the world and how we get rid of it. If appropriate, ask the children what is wrong with our world, a messy world into which Jesus was born. This will connect with the Golden nuggets verses later.

On the Jesus Quest

1 Landlubbers song
(5 minutes)

If the majority of your group are familiar with the song because they attended a *Landlubbers* holiday club, go straight into it! If it's new, teach it to your group if you think it's appropriate. You'll find it on the *Light for Everyone* CD (SU, 1 84427 080 7).

⊕2 Landlubbers arrive in town
(15 minutes)

What you need

- The Captains' story for this session (see page 33)
- *The Jesus Quest* DVD and TV/projector
- The clue for next session, written on a scroll (see page 19)

What you do

Sit the children down so they can see both you and the television/screen. Remind everyone of this session's clue and read the Captains' story (Landlubbers arrive in town, page 33). It leads straight into episode 1 of *The Jesus Quest* DVD. As you continue the story after the DVD, produce the next clue at the right time.

⊕3 The real story
⊕ *(10 minutes)*

What you need

- Bible, or copy of Luke 2:1–14 from page 15
- A selection of old Christmas cards, including secular ones and some of shepherds, angels, Mary, Joseph, Jesus and the stable (you do not need any wise men pictures)

What you do

Read Luke 2:1–14. Spread the Christmas cards among the children and invite them to choose cards which depict something from the Bible passage as you are reading it. Which cards have made things up? Which cards (if any!) best show what the Bible says really happened.

⊕4 Good news headlines
⊕ *(15 minutes)*

What you need

- The six headlines from page 23, written on separate pieces of paper
- Large sheets of white paper
- Writing and drawing materials
- A4 paper
- Glue sticks

What you do

Divide the children into groups of not more than six. Get each group to choose one of the headlines. Ask an adult or confident child to read the Bible passage that goes with the chosen headline. The group then compiles a newspaper front page to go with it. Each child can draw a picture or write a comment and stick it on. Share the different pages together. What have the groups found out about Jesus? Remember, some children will have very little knowledge of Jesus. Take this opportunity to chat about what the children have found out and what they think so far.

You could display these front pages over the next few weeks to remind the children. They may prompt passing adults to pray for you!

⊕5 Who am I?
(10 minutes)

What you need

- Appropriate headgear for each of the characters
- Willing leaders, or children who are confident readers
- The clues written on individual cards
- Mock microphone
- Characters and clues from page 23

What you do

This activity should help children identify with the different characters in the story and develop the clues concept, which is core to *Clues2Use*. Dress each character (Mary, Shepherd, Anna, Teacher of the Law, John the Baptist, Member of the synagogue congregation) appropriately. The characters take it in turns to read their clues and have their identity guessed. If the children need more clues, each character can then be asked a question or two, using the microphone. If you have limited time or volunteers, you could miss out the Teacher of the Law and the Member of the synagogue congregation.

In the treasure chest

⊕1 Landlubbers cafe
(5–10 minutes)

What you need

- Angel Delight-type dessert, enough for some per child
- Plates and teaspoons
- Toppings eg sprinkles, cherries, chocolate chips, mini marshmallows, wafers

What you do

To link with this session's theme, serve the Angel Delight dessert and ask the children to shape the dessert into an angel shape. Provide the toppings so the group can decorate their angel shapes and have fun looking at everyone's

Checklist

- Clue cards (see page 18), today's clue (see page 19), glue sticks, pencils
- A collection of junk and a graffiti wall to set the scene
- *The Jesus Quest* DVD and television/projector
- 'Landlubbers arrive in town' story (see page 33)
- A scroll with the clue for next session written on
- Materials for your choice of activities for *Give us a clue*, *On the Jesus Quest* and *In the treasure chest*

⊕ *When you see this logo, the activity is particularly appropriate for smaller groups.*

⊕ *When you see this logo, the activity will work well with older children.*

⊕ *When you see this logo, the activity is key to the session.*

1

efforts. Then have fun eating it! As you eat, encourage the children to talk about angels and the part they played in the Christmas story.

The Angel Delight was very popular at the Hothouse. The children made their own – and loved it, but it did make it quite a long activity.

2 QUEStion time
(10–15 minutes)

What you need
- A 'treasure chest'-style box
- Pieces of paper and pencils

What you do
Sit the children down in a comfortable place and talk about how Jesus asked lots of questions of the teachers of the Law in the temple. Ask the children what they would like to ask about God. Get them to write their questions down, helping those who need it (or scribing for them) and post their questions in the treasure chest. Take them out and all share in answering them.

This is early in the programme and some children may find it hard to think of what they would like to ask God. Give them some ideas from your own experience. However, children who have been to *Landlubbers* or have been at your club for some time may be very comfortable with this idea.

3 Design your own Christmas card *(15 minutes)*

What you need
- Rough paper
- Good quality paper or card (A4 size folded)
- Drawing and colouring materials

What you do
Remind the children of the Luke 2 passage you read earlier and the Christmas cards that you looked at. Tell them that now it's their turn to design a card that tells the real story or part of it. They can try out their ideas on the rough paper first. Talk together about what the Christmas story means to you as you create your cards. Remember that some children really lack confidence when asked to draw so give lots of encouragement. Enjoy sharing the finished cards together.

This activity particularly follows on well from *On the Jesus Quest* 'The real story'.

4 Good news graffiti
(15 minutes)

What you need
- Long piece of paper (lining paper is ideal) taped to the wall or the floor
- Paint or thick markers in a variety of colours

What you do
Get the children to write out Luke 2:14 (as much as is appropriate and in their own words if possible) as the 'Good news' verse which they can stick on the graffiti wall. If the children have any other linked phrases or pictures they would like to add, let them do so. What would they sing to announce that Jesus has been born?

5 Golden nugget verses
(5 minutes)

Philippians 2:6,7 are our special verses for sessions 1 to 4. In each session, one of the activities will be connected with them. For this first session, write the verses on a piece of card and place the card by the junk models the children made earlier (if you did *Give us a clue* 'Scrap Art'). Read the verses and explain very briefly that Jesus came into all the mess and junk of the world to show us how much he loves us. Remember that Philippians was the central Bible book in the *Landlubbers* holiday club programme with the memory verse being Philippians 3:8. The golden nugget verses will continue to make this connection but make sense whether or not you have used *Landlubbers*.

Extra for afterwards
Maybe there is something you and your group could do to share Jesus' light in your community, eg carol singing, painting a colourful mural (with permission!) on a wall that has been used for graffiti.

For several years now, the local churches have been carol singing on the estate where the Hothouse is. An exciting development of the past two Christmases is that the Hothouse children have really taken over this event. They lead us round the streets at a cracking pace and know exactly where they want to sing!

1

⊕ Captains' story: Landlubbers arrive in town

There are pirates in the city! Pirates in the town! But don't be alarmed. These pirates are not going to cause any harm. Captains Yo-ho and Heave-ho are Landlubbers now. For many months they were shipwrecked on a tropical island and while they were there, they made some amazing discoveries about a friend of Jesus named Paul. They decided that they'd like to follow Jesus too – which is brilliant news! They still don't know much about him though, and that's why they've left the peace and tranquillity of the island and arrived on the mainland. They are Landlubbers on the Jesus Quest. They've already found themselves at the cinema where they thoroughly enjoyed watching *(Name a children's film which is currently running at the cinema.)* and received their first clue. Let's join them now. We're on the Jesus Quest too.

The two Captains read their clue again. The street they stood in was covered with litter. There was graffiti on the walls and a homeless man huddled in his sleeping bag. A group of children were playing football with an old drinks can and a huge dog licked his lips as he saw Heave-ho's parrot.

'Are you sure we're in the right place?' whispered Heave-ho uneasily.

'We must be,' answered Yo-ho. 'We need to find an empty house with broken windows. None of the other streets had anything like that in them did they? This one does. Look, what about that house over there? It's completely abandoned. No one's lived in there for ages. Come on!'

Reluctantly, Heave-ho followed Yo-ho through the overgrown garden into the tumbledown house beyond. The broken front door opened easily. The house smelt damp and mouldy.

'I don't know how we're going to discover anything about Jesus here,' grumbled Heave-ho. 'For a start, we need to find out where he was born and all that kind of thing. It certainly can't have been anywhere like this so…'

'Shhh!' said Yo-ho, suddenly. 'Look what Nelson's found!'

Nelson the parrot was perched on top of a television and DVD player in the corner of the room. He was looking very pleased with himself.

'What a weird thing to find in a run-down house,' said Heave-ho, switching it on.

Show episode 1 of The Jesus Quest DVD at this point. (Timings for The Jesus Quest video for this episode are 0.30 to 7.40.)

'So now we know!' said Yo-ho quietly, after watching exactly what we've watched today.

'Jesus – the one who God promised to send to us, really was born in a place a bit like this; not on a beautiful desert island or in a posh palace, but in a dirty, old stable in an ordinary town.'

'Makes you think, doesn't it,' agreed Heave-ho. 'He came to bring good news to the poor; good news to the people who live in this street and streets like it everywhere. That means everyone can get to know him. I'm glad we didn't stay on that island. Let's find out what he did next! Where's the next clue?'

Nelson was perching on something again. This time it was a scroll nestling in a cobwebby corner. The pirates opened it and read:

'Changing rooms and lots of noise,
Lifeguards with their whistles poised.
Water sparkling blue and green,
We even have a wave machine.'

Tuned in – prayer activities

Include this prayer activity somewhere in your programme.
(10 minutes)

Light of the world
What you need
- A large map of your town/village/area (you could draw this out in chalk or tape on the floor)
- A nightlight (in a safe holder) for each child
- Matches (kept by you!)

What you do
Sit the children in a circle with the map in the centre. When the children are settled give each one a nightlight. Only light them if you are sure the children are calm enough. Ask each child to put their light on whatever part of the map they would like to – maybe the street they live in. Pray a short prayer asking that Jesus, the light of the world, may shine his light and love into the places the children have put their nightlights. You could also add that we too, with Jesus' love in us, can be like lights, and close by reading Philippians 2:15b,16. 'Try to shine as lights among the people of this world, as you hold firmly to the message that gives life.' (These are the key verses in session 3 of the *Landlubbers* holiday club programme.)

Session 2

Luke
5:1–11,27–32

Aim To discover that when Jesus said, 'Follow me!', all kinds of people found that they wanted to do just that.

To explore what it was that made Jesus such a good leader and know that we can make a choice to follow him too.

Notes for you

Jesus made a big impact on Simon Peter and Matthew (Levi) when he asked them to follow him. Simon recognised something of his total goodness and Matthew (Levi) saw that he cared about him, in spite of his job and the sort of company he kept. Pray that Jesus will make an impact on the children this session, and that they will think about what it might mean to let him be their leader.

Be aware that this may be very new language to children who are new to the club. Don't talk to a child about Jesus being their leader unless you know they understand.

The Jesus Quest episode includes: the call of Peter, Jairus' daughter, the call of Matthew, the naming of the twelve disciples.

The key story is the call of Peter.

Landlubbers
go to the swimming pool

Give us a clue

Welcome the children and give them their clue card and today's clue (about the swimming pool) to stick on to it. Help the children read the clue so they remember where the Landlubbers will be going today. Then collect in the clue cards ready for next time.

All these fun swimming activities will not only introduce the swimming theme but also prepare the children to hear the stories of Jesus and the fishermen.

⊜1 Dry land swimming
(10 minutes)

What you do

Divide the group into teams of four and line them up at one end of the room. Tell the teams they have to run to the other end of the room and back, while doing the arm actions from a particular swimming stroke. The first person 'swims' using breaststroke arm actions, the second person using crawl, the third backstroke and the fourth butterfly. You may have to demonstrate if some children are unsure as to which is which. Make sure there are no obstacles in the way for anyone 'swimming' backwards. The winning team is the one to complete the 'medley' first!

⊜2 Ready to swim
(10 minutes)

What you need

• A set of swimming related items (eg large trunks/costume, goggles, swimming hat, towel, flippers, armbands, swim ring, float/beach ball) for each team.

What you do

Divide the group into teams (if you have a small group, you could do this activity against the clock). Choose one person per team to be 'dressed' for swimming (maybe someone who

Jesus – the leader

doesn't like running or is unable to run). Team members take it in turns to run to the other end of the playing space and pick up an item of swimwear. They should put it on if they can and then return to the rest of their team. They should then take it off and put it on the team member they're dressing up. The first team to dress their 'swimmer' with all the items is the winner.

☺ The Hothouse children loved this game and one girl wore her swimming hat for the rest of the evening! ☺

⊜3 Designer swimwear
(10 minutes)

What you need

• Sheets of coloured paper cut into swimming shorts or a tankini top shape (see page 20)
• Felt-tip pens, paints or scraps of fabric, glue

What you do

Ask the children to design swimwear for Captains Yo-ho and Heave-ho. These could either be small ones based on the template on page 20 or large ones for a life-sized pirate.

⊜4 Goldfish race
(10 minutes)

What you need

• Two buckets or bowls for each team
• A disposable plastic cup for each child
• Carrots chopped up into sticks (these are your goldfish!)
• Water!

What you do

Divide the group into teams and give each person a plastic cup. Put a container of water with the 'goldfish' in it at the front of each line and an empty container at the end. The person at the front of the line scoops up a cup of water, including one 'goldfish'. They then pour the water and 'goldfish' into the cup of the next person in the team and so on down the line. The person at the end tips the 'goldfish'and water into the empty container and goes to the front of the line to start the process again. The team with the most goldfish (and water, if you like) wins.

Play this game outside if possible, as there is likely to be some spillage. Encourage the children to walk from the back of the line to the front, to avoid slipping.

On the Jesus Quest

⊕1 Landlubbers and Clues2Use songs *(2 minutes)*

Sing the *Landlubbers* song at this point if you're using it. Introduce the *Clues2Use* song this week.

⊕2 Landlubbers go to the swimming pool *(15 minutes)*

What you need
- The Captains' story for this session (see page 37)
- *The Jesus Quest* DVD and TV/projector
- The clue for next session, written on an old/cheap towel (see page 19)

What you do
Sit the children down so they can see both you and the television/screen. Remind everyone of this session's clue and read the Captains' story (Landlubbers go to the swimming pool, page 37). It leads straight into episode 2 of *The Jesus Quest* DVD. As you continue the story after the DVD, produce the next clue at the right time.

⊕3 Follow me – Call of Simon Peter *(10 minutes)*

What you need
- Bibles or copies of Luke 5:1–11 from page 15
- Plastic netting (from a garden centre)
- Hundreds of fish shapes cut out of newspaper
- Chairs
- A pot containing pieces of paper, each with the name of a character (Jesus, Simon Peter, Andrew, James, John) from the passage written on it

What you do
Arrange chairs to make two boats. Get the children to pick a name from the pot so they know which character they are. (The remaining children can be the crowd by the lake, but if you have a large number of children divide them into two groups so that as many as possible can be involved. Alternatively, one group could do 'Follow me – Call of Matthew'.) Read Luke 5:1–11 slowly and clearly, so that the children can act it simply as you do.

The Hothouse children really enjoyed this activity. A 10-year-old who is a confident reader read the passage for the rest to act to and was very pleased with her role.

⊕4 Follow me – Call of Matthew *(10 minutes)*

What you need
- Bibles or copies of Luke 5:27–32 from page 15
- Coins (chocolate, gold card or real!)
- Table and chair for Levi
- Table and chairs, paper plates and cups for dinner guests
- A pot containing pieces of paper, each with the name of a character (Jesus, Levi, guests, teachers of the Law) from the passage written on it

What you do
Arrange the props and proceed as in 'Follow Me – Call of Simon Peter'. If you have different groups who have worked on these two activities, then encourage each group to act out their story for the others.

⊕4 Follow Me – The J team *(10 minutes)*

What you need
- Bible
- The names of the twelve disciples (as listed in Luke 6:14–16) written out on individual pieces of card and placed around the room

What you do
Either you or a child who is a confident reader should read Luke 6:12–16. Every time a name is mentioned, the children should get up and look around the room to see who can find the name and bring it back. At the end of the passage you should have the names of all Jesus' disciples.

Checklist
- Clue cards, today's clue (see page 19), glue sticks
- A selection of swimming rings, armbands, swimming goggles, towels etc to set the scene
- *The Jesus Quest* DVD and television/projector
- Next session's clue written on an old/cheap swimming towel
- 'Landlubbers go to the swimming pool' story (see page 37)
- Materials for your choice of activities for *Give us a clue*, *On the Jesus Quest* and *In the treasure chest*

When you see this logo, the activity is particularly appropriate for smaller groups.

When you see this logo, the activity will work well with older children.

When you see this logo, the activity is key to the session.

2

In the treasure chest

This is an opportunity for you to talk from personal experience about what it means to follow Jesus. Think beforehand what you might say (see page 12).

⊕1 Landlubbers cafe
(10 minutes)

What you need
- A small portion of fish and chips for everyone (either from a local chippy if this is convenient or cooked on the premises if this is possible)

What you do
Serve the food to the children, making sure you have alternatives for any children who don't like fish. Enjoy this time of chatting and eating together, making sure you chat about the stories you have explored today and what the children think about them.

⊙ *The Hothouse is very conveniently situated next door to The Orange Chippy and, believe it or not, the chips really are orange. I don't know the recipe but the chips are very popular!* ⊙

⊕2 QUESTion time
(10 minutes)

What you do
If you had a QUESTion time activity last week, you may want to make it a regular feature throughout the series. Invite children to bring questions with them each week for the treasure chest. At this point in the session, take the questions out and answer them together.

⊕3 Follow the Leader
⊕ *(10 minutes)*

What you do
Sit the children in a circle and ask for a volunteer. The volunteer must try to guess who the leader is out of the people sitting in the circle. The volunteer leaves the room briefly while rest of the group decides on a leader. When the volunteer returns, the leader must lead everyone else in actions, eg clapping, hopping on the spot, waving arms. They should change the actions from time to time. The volunteer must guess who the leader is.

After playing the game with different volunteers, talk about what makes a good leader in real life. Why did the disciples want to follow Jesus? How was he a good leader?

⊕4 Fishing net
(15 minutes)

What you need
- A variety of fish-shaped cards – including seahorses and eels (see page 20)
- Collage materials, eg gold and silver scales, sequins, wiggly eyes, craft pom-poms, pipe cleaners, felt-tip pens
- Glue, scissors, sticky tape, Blu-Tack
- A net stuck or drawn onto a large piece of paper

What you do
Ask the children to decorate a fish shape as creatively as they can. When they are ready, put them inside the net. Let the children decide if they are going to be at the top or the bottom or stuck in a hole. As you do this, talk about what Jesus might have meant when he said to his disciples that they were going to bring in people instead of fish (Luke 5:10). What might it mean to be caught, or to belong to Jesus? This is an opportunity for you to explain what it means to you to be a friend of Jesus. Do make sure that no child leaves with the impression that by using the fishing and net image, you are saying that people are trapped into becoming Jesus' friends. His disciples had the choice in this story.

⊕5 Golden nugget verses
(10 minutes)

What you need
- Fish shapes cut out of brightly coloured card
- Felt-tip pens
- The words of Philippians 2:6,7 written individually on small pieces of paper

What you do
Give each child a word (or two, depending on the size of your group) and a fish (or two!). Ask the children to write their word on their fish and decorate it. Stick the fish around the room in the right order and read the golden nugget verses.

Extra for afterwards
You could arrange a trip to a local swimming pool with your group and their families.

⊕ Captains' story: Landlubbers go to the swimming pool

'So we've got to go to the swimming pool,' said Captain Heave-ho, scratching his head. 'That's an odd place for the Jesus Quest to be taking us, isn't it?'

'That's what we thought about the house,' chuckled Yo-ho.

'True enough,' agreed Heave-ho. 'Have you ever been to a swimming pool before?'

'Never,' said Yo-ho. 'The open sea is more my scene. Can you swim, Heave-ho?'

'Swim? Of course I can swim! Whoever heard of a pirate who can't sw— well, actually, no, I can't. I always dreaded having to walk the plank. Can you?'

'No.'

'Well, we'll learn together then,' said Heave-ho, far more cheerfully than he felt. 'Come on!'

Yo-ho and Heave-ho eventually arrived at the pool. They were quite surprised to find that it was indoors, and they were rather embarrassed by the way everyone seemed to be staring and pointing at them.

'Haven't you ever seen pirates before?' growled Heave-ho, as he carefully climbed down the steps into the water.

Well, nobody had seen pirates before, especially not pirates in red and white spotted swimming gear which came down to their knees, armbands to keep them afloat and goggles and flippers which they felt made them look like professional divers. Heave-ho even had Nelson the parrot perched on his head. What's more, they had somehow ended up in the middle of a swimming lesson. There was nothing for it but to join in. They listened obediently to the instructor and by the end of the session had begun to enjoy themselves. Yo-ho had even taken one armband off.

'See you next week,' said the instructor, as they climbed out of the pool. 'It won't be long before you're swimming like fish!'

'Talking of fish,' said Heave-ho to Yo-ho, 'I'm starving! Shall we get some fish and chips on the way home?'

'Good idea,' answered Yo-ho, 'and we'll watch the next part of *The Jesus Quest* DVD too.'

Show episode 2 of The Jesus Quest *DVD at this point. (Timings for* The Jesus Quest *video for this episode are 7.40 to 14.55.)*

'Wonder if Jesus could swim, then?' said Yo-ho as they switched off the DVD player.

'Probably,' answered Heave-ho. 'After all, we've just seen him in that fishing boat. Wasn't it amazing how Simon Peter and all the others left what they were doing and followed him?'

'Yeah – and how that man, Jairus, knew he could help his daughter. Jesus was a good leader, wasn't he? Gave everyone a kind of confidence in him.'

'A bit like with our swimming you mean? We tried something new today and our swimming instructor gave us the confidence we needed.'

'Yeah! It's not just swimming though. Jesus will give us the confidence to do lots of new things for him if we follow him – just like he did with Simon Peter and the others.'

'I'm tired now,' yawned Heave-ho. 'I'll just hang my swimming towel up to dry before bed. Ohhh! Look! The next clue.'

And sure enough, there it was, written on Heave-ho's swimming towel. Together the pirates read:

'A building where you go to learn,
Though some can't wait till end of term!
Landlubbers, do your very best
On the next part of the Jesus Quest.'

Tuned in – prayer activities

Include this prayer idea somewhere in your session. *(10 minutes)*

Flower prayers
What you need
- Paper water lilies or fish (see pages 20 and 21 – enough for two for each child)
- Shallow bowls of water
- Pencils

What you do
Give out the water lilies or fish, and ask the children to think of a leader they know or have heard of and write their name in the middle of a water lily/fish. Then ask them to fold the petals/fins, head and tail over the name and place the water lily/fish carefully on the water. Pray that these leaders may be open to God leading them and watch! The

petals/fins will gradually open. The children may like to write their own names on the second water lily/fish and pray that they too may be open to God and to following Jesus.

You could close by reading Philippians 1:9,10a

'I pray that your love will keep on growing and that you will fully know and understand how to make the right choices.'

Landlubbers
go to school

Aim **To show that Jesus was a brilliant teacher and is well worth listening to (even the wind and waves listened to him!)**
To begin to understand how, if we let his words go deep inside us, we will want to respond with our lives.

Notes for you

Listening to Jesus and letting his words go deep inside us are important if we are going to let him change us – the woman with the perfume discovered this. The parable of the sower is also about listening to him and letting him grow deep, strong roots in our lives. Pray for the children in your group who find it hard to listen to anyone. Pray that the Holy Spirit will begin to calm their storms as they hear about Jesus' love and forgiveness. Pray that you may be a good listener to the children in your group.

The Jesus Quest episode includes: parts of the Sermon on the Mount, the woman and the perfume, the parable of the sower, the storm on the lake.

The key story is the parable of the sower.

Give us a clue

Welcome the children and give them their clue card and today's clue (about going to school) to stick on. (Have some spares ready, in case any new children come.) Help the children to read the clue so they remember where the Landlubbers will be going today. Then collect in the clue cards ready for next time.

⊜1 Parachute games
(15 minutes)

What you need
- A parachute (if you don't have one it is very likely that a local school, after-school club or another church will – they are also available from Scripture Union)
- Foam balls

What you do
Make sure you are familiar with some basic parachute games such as 'Categories' (running under) and 'Cat and Mouse'. Enjoy playing the games together. Explain the instructions clearly and remind the children of the importance of listening. If you use the chute again later, in conjunction with On the Jesus Quest 'Storm on the Lake', the children will be familiar with it and will be happy to use it for a 'story' rather than a game.

⊜2 Opposites
 (10 minutes)

What you need
- Pieces of card
- Marker pen

What you do
Before the session, write out pairs of opposites on the pieces of card (one word per card). Opposites could include: loud/quiet, poor/rich, sad/happy, stormy/calm, guilty/innocent, accuse/forgive, dirty/clean, selfish/generous, wise/foolish, awake/asleep. Using two different

Jesus – the teacher

colours of card makes the game quicker and easier.

Ask the children to sit in a circle with the words face down in the middle. The children take it in turns to turn over two words (one of each colour card, if you've used two colours). If they pick up a pair of opposite words, they keep the cards; if not, they are turned back over. Continue until all the opposites have been collected.

The opposites are relevant to the stories of the storm on the lake, and the woman and the perfume. They illustrate that listening to Jesus can make a big difference.

⊜3 You choose!
(15 minutes)

What you need
- Four tables
- Ping-pong balls
- Paint and washing-up liquid mixture (blue and green) in plastic tubs, with straws
- White A4 paper
- 'Magic' drawing slates (the sort that rub out when you pull the tab at the top)
- Seeds to plant, plus compost, flowerpots, sticky labels (or shallow trays, cotton wool, cress seed; or seed trays, compost, grass seed)

What you do
Set out tables for the four activities below:
Blow football – two children at a time, one either end of a table – see who can blow the ping-pong ball off the table first.
Bubble printing – the children blow through the straw into the paint and washing-up liquid mixture until large bubbles form. Then they place a piece of paper on top of the bubbles to make a print.
'Magic' slates – the children can draw and rub out as many times as they like.
Seed planting – talk about growing conditions as the children plant.

Explain the activities to the children and let them move around the tables choosing their activities. Make sure there is an adult at each table to guide and encourage the children.

The blow football and bubble printing connect with the storm on the lake, the magic slates with the woman and the perfume and the seed planting with the parable of the sower – all feature in this episode of *The Jesus Quest*.

🙂 *Blow football was a particular success at the Hothouse!* 🙂

On the Jesus Quest

⊕1 Landlubbers and Clues2Use songs *(2 minutes)*

Sing the *Landlubbers* song and/or the *Clues2Use* song at this point, if you're using them.

⊕2 Landlubbers go to school
(15 minutes)

What you need
- The Captains' story for session 3 (see page 41)
- *The Jesus Quest* DVD and TV/projector
- The clue for next session (see page 19), printed out in a 'computer' style

What you do
Sit the children down so they can see both you and the television/screen. Remind everyone of this session's clue and read the Captains' story (Landlubbers go to school). It leads straight into episode 3 of *The Jesus Quest* DVD. As you continue the story after the DVD, produce the next clue at the right time.

⊕3 A seedy story – the parable of the sower ⊕ *(10 minutes)*

What you need
- Bible or copy of Luke 8:4–8 from page 16
- A packet of sunflower seeds
- Four seed trays:
  One with gravel in it (path)
  One with large stones and a thin layer of soil (rocky ground)
  One with soil sprinkled with dandelion/thistle seeds (ground with thorn bushes)
  One with good, rich compost (good ground)

What you do
Ask the children to sit in a circle with the four seed trays in the centre. Give each child a few sunflower seeds to hold. Slowly read the parable of the sower, indicating which children are to put their seeds in the appropriate seed tray. At the end of the story ask the children where they would like their seeds to be. Ask if anyone can remember what Jesus said the story means (from watching *The Jesus Quest*). What kind of soil would we like to be? Why?

⊕4 Storm on the lake
(10 minutes)

What you need
- Parachute
- Bible

What you do
Slowly read the story of Jesus calming the storm on the lake (Luke 8:22–25), giving the children the opportunity to act out the story using the parachute, making big waves when appropriate and holding it still when the water is calm. Repeat the passage a few times.

In the treasure chest

⊖1 Landlubbers cafe
(10 minutes)

What you need
- A selection of fruits (if you use fruits with plenty of seeds, like melons, you could use them for *Give us a clue* 'You choose')

What you do
Share the fruit together, encouraging the children to try something new. Talk about what the fruit tastes like and see if the children have found a new fruit that they like. Use this refreshment time to chat to the children about what they think of the stories they have been exploring. What do they think of Jesus? What do they think of the chance to become his friend?

⊖2 QUESTion time
(10 minutes)

What you do
Check the treasure chest for new questions and answer them together. Remember to encourage the children to put questions they would like to ask in the chest. Make sure you include everyone in your discussions as you answer the questions.

Checklist
- Clue cards, today's clue (see page 19), glue sticks
- Tables and chair, books and other school equipment to set the scene
- *The Jesus Quest* DVD and television/ projector
- Next week's clue printed out so that it has obviously come from a computer
- 'Landlubbers go to school' story (see page 41)
- Materials for your choice of activities for *Give us a clue*, *On the Jesus Quest* and *In the treasure chest*

⊕ *When you see this logo, the activity is particularly appropriate for smaller groups.*

☺ *When you see this logo, the activity will work well with older children.*

⊕ *When you see this logo, the activity is key to the session.*

3

H3 Grow bag quiz
(15 minutes)

What you need
- Six strips of card of equal length, taped together so they lie, concertinaed, on top of each other, with a paper flower stuck at the end of the top strip
- A bag containing pictures of the sun, a watering can, a bird, a snail, a box of compost, weed killer, a thistle, a slug

What you do
Divide the children into two teams. Ask each team in turn, a question based on this session's Bible passage. If they answer their question correctly, they can pick a picture from the 'grow bag'. If it's something that will help their flower to grow extend it by one stem length. Sample questions (for the Parable of the Sower):
- What two things happened to the seed that fell on the path? *It was trodden on and birds ate it.*
- Why didn't the seed that fell on the stony ground grow for long? *It didn't have deep roots and the sun scorched it.*
- What did the thorn bushes do to the seeds that grew there? *Choked them.*
- What happened to the seeds that fell on good soil? *They grew and produced a good harvest.*
- What did Jesus say the seed in his story was like? *His Word/message.*
- What happens to people who hear Jesus' message but don't let it grow strong roots in their lives? *They give up when life gets hard.*
- What happens to people who let riches and pleasure become more important than Jesus' message? *They stop growing.*
- What happens to people who listen to Jesus' message and let it grow in their lives? *They keep growing and have good fruit.*
- Why didn't Captain Yo-ho want to go to school? *She'd never been before.*
- Why was the head teacher pleased to see Yo-ho and Heave-ho? *Because it was Pirate Day.*

H4 Double bubble
(15 minutes)

What you need
- The bubble prints done earlier in *Give us a clue* 'You choose'
- Dark-coloured paper for a background
- A picture of a boat
- Paper speech bubbles
- Paper, drawing materials and glue

What you do
Stick the bubble prints onto the background paper to form the sea and then add the empty boat. Ask the children to draw a disciple each (or Jesus) to stick in the boat, and then give each child a paper speech bubble so that they can write something their disciple (or Jesus) is saying. The speech bubbles can then also be stuck on the collage. (If you have a large group, some children could be working on the sea and background, while others are drawing disciples and others who like writing are working on the speech bubbles.)

H5 Golden nugget verses
(10 minutes)

What you need
- Black paper and coloured chalks

What you do
If you haven't focused on an activity using Philippians 2:6,7 in previous sessions, give the children black paper and coloured chalks so that they can each write a phrase and decorate it. Stick the verses around the room and say them through a couple of times. Can any of the children learn them by the next session?

Extra for afterwards
You and your group could run a stall at your local school's summer or Christmas fair, especially if your children come mostly from one school.

Tuned in – prayer activities

Choose one or both of the ideas here and opposite. *(10 minutes)*

School prayers
What you need
- A paper person per child
- Pencils

What you do
Ask the children to think of an adult who works at their school who they'd like to pray for, eg teacher or classroom assistant. Ask them to write the person's name on the paper shape and place it in the middle of the circle. Pray for these people, and also for the children, especially any who find school difficult.

You could close by saying the words of Philippians 4:6:
'Don't worry about anything, but pray about everything. With thankful hearts offer up your prayers and requests to God.'
(This is the key verse in session 5 of the *Landlubbers* holiday club programme.)

⊕ Captains' story: Landlubbers go to school

'School?' said Captain Yo-ho, shaking her head. 'I don't think so! A swimming pool is one thing but school is quite another!'

'Oh, I don't know,' said Heave-ho. 'I quite liked school myself.'

'I never went to school,' admitted Yo-ho.

'Well then, how do you know you don't like it? Come on. Yo-ho, polish your earring. We'd better look smart!'

But when they reached the gates of the local primary school an amazing sight met their eyes. Dozens of children were arriving, dressed exactly like them! There were eye patches, stripy T-shirts, shoes with silver buckles, pirate captain's hats, gold earrings and brightly coloured toy parrots.

'Welcome to our school Pirates Day!' announced a carefully coloured sign. The children crowded around Yo-ho and Heave-ho.

'Wow! No one told us there'd be real pirates at school today!'

'Does your parrot talk?'

'Have you ever had to walk the plank?'

'Do you have your own ship?'

The questions were endless! The head teacher looked a bit uncertain of these real pirates but she invited them in. She kept close to them all the time they were in the school.

Yo-ho and Heave-ho spent an interesting time being interviewed and drawn. They told stories about famous pirates from history. The children were fascinated.

'Would you like a school dinner?' asked the headteacher. The captains had never had pizza before, but when they tried it, they loved it!

'Plenty of fruit for pudding,' said the head. 'We don't want you getting scurvy!'

After lunch, two of the mini-pirates were brought in from the playground looking rather the worse for wear.

'They've been fighting,' said the dinner lady.

'Well,' shouted one of the young pirates, 'that's what pirates do! You don't expect pirates to be friends do you? Anyway, he started it!'

'We used to be like that,' said Heave-ho to the two boys, 'but we decided to have a new start. We forgave each other. We don't fight any more – it doesn't get you anywhere. Being friends is much better.'

During the afternoon, Yo-ho was given a science lesson and Heave-ho tried out the computer.

'I didn't know school could be so much fun,' said Yo-ho, as they settled down to watch the next episode of *The Jesus Quest* that night.

Show episode 3 of The Jesus Quest *DVD at this point. (Timings for* The Jesus Quest *video for this episode are 14.55 to 21.48.)*

'Jesus was an excellent teacher then,' commented Yo-ho, as she watched Nelson switch off the DVD player with his beak.

'He really knew his stuff, didn't he? And it all makes so much sense,' said Heave-ho thoughtfully.

'I really like that story he told about the farmer planting those seeds; and being in the boat in that storm would have been really scary. I used to get seasick on my ship and that was loads bigger. Good thing Jesus was there. I wonder where the next clue is?!'

Heave-ho smiled, 'Look! I've printed it out. It appeared on the computer screen at school this afternoon.'

'Did it? Let's see!'

'Checkouts, music, special offers,
Rushing, dreaming mass of shoppers.
So much choice down every aisle,
Then stand and queue for half a mile!'

Tuned in – prayer activities

'Magic' slate prayer

What you need
- The 'magic' slates used in *Give us a clue* 'You choose'

What you do
Remind the children of the activity they did earlier – drawing on the slates and rubbing out. Refer to the woman who poured perfume on Jesus' feet, seen in this session's episode of *The Jesus Quest* DVD. She knew she was forgiven by Jesus – we too can have a new start with Jesus. Invite the children to write down anything they really want to say 'sorry' for and then watch it disappear as they rub it out. When Jesus forgives us he 'rubs out' the things we are sorry about and gives us a new start.

Luke
9:10–17

Aim **To enjoy the fact that Jesus is surprising! He didn't always do what people expected him to and he can do more than we can ever imagine.**

Landlubbers
go to the supermarket

Notes for you

When 5,000 people were hungry, Jesus surprised everyone by feeding them all (and having plenty left over). His story about the man who was mugged had a surprising ending. No one expected him to invite himself to Zacchaeus' house or to say that they all needed to become like children. Pray that the children will be excited as they discover what a surprising friend Jesus can be; and pray that you as leaders will let yourselves be surprised by Jesus all over again.

The Jesus Quest episode includes: Jesus feeding 5,000 people, the parable of the good Samaritan, 'Come like a child', the healing of the blind man, Zacchaeus.

 The key story is Jesus feeds a hungry crowd.

Give us a clue

Welcome the children and give them their clue card and today's clue (about the supermarket) to stick on to it. Help the children read the clue, so they remember where the Landlubbers will be going today. Then collect in the clue cards ready for next time. Each Give us a clue activity explores food and where it comes from.

1 Supermarket dash
 (10 minutes)

What you need
- A selection of shopping items, eg tins, packets, loaves of bread, plastic bottles of squash, unsquashable fruit and veg
- Two supermarket style baskets (or two trolleys, if your venue is large enough and you are close to a friendly supermarket!)

What you do
Divide the children into two teams and line them up at one end of the room. Put the shopping items at the other end. Give the first person in each team an empty basket or trolley. Team members take it in turns to run to the 'supermarket', put one item in the basket, then run back. They should pass the basket to the next person and go to the back of the line. The next person then goes to the 'supermarket', and so on. At the end of your allotted time, the teams count how many items they have in their basket.

> *We played this twice at the Hothouse, but I think the children would have happily carried on all evening!*

2 Little Ern goes shopping
(10 minutes)

What you do
Line up the children in teams and give each child the name of an item of shopping (each team needs to be given the same names). Place chairs

Jesus – full of surprises

at the other end of your playing space, one in front of each team and get an adult to sit on each chair to anchor it! Make up a simple story about 'Little Ern' going shopping, naming all the items regularly. When a child hears their item mentioned, they should run to the chair, go around it and then back to their place. When 'Little Ern' is mentioned, the whole team runs together but must stay in a line. The first team/member back each time gets a point for their team.

3 Alphabetti spaghetti
(10 minutes)

What you need
- A tin of alphabetti spaghetti for each group of about six
- A tray or baking sheet for each group
- A paper plate for each child
- Teaspoons

What you do
Divide the children into groups and give each group a tin of alphabetti spaghetti, a tray to spread the letters out on and a paper plate for each child. Everyone in the group must try and make their name from the spaghetti letters. See which group is the first to complete their names.

Handwashing facilities will be needed afterwards!

4 Bread making
(15 minutes)

What you need
- A packet of bread mix for each group of six
- Extra flour
- A mixing bowl, baking tray, wooden spoon and water, for each group

What you do
Divide the children into groups of no more than six, each with a leader. Ask the groups to make up the bread mix, following the directions on the packet.

If you have access to an oven, and a long enough period of time for the dough to rise, bake the bread for the children to take home. Otherwise the children can take their bread home to bake. Remember to write down clear instructions if they do this. Remember food hygiene and health and safety rules.

On the Jesus Quest

⊕1 Landlubbers and Clues2Use songs *(2 minutes)*

Sing the *Landlubbers* song and/or the *Clues2Use* song at this point, if you're using them.

⊕2 Landlubbers go to the supermarket *(15 minutes)*

What you need
- The Captains' story for this session (see page 45)
- *The Jesus Quest* DVD and TV/projector
- The clue for next session (see page 19), written on the back of a cereal packet

What you do
Sit the children down so they can see both you and the television/screen. Remind everyone of this session's clue and read the Captains' story (Landlubbers go to the supermarket). It leads straight into episode 4 of *The Jesus Quest* DVD. As you continue the story after the DVD, produce the next clue at the right time. For the clue, create a packet of 'Frostabix' by designing a logo and sticking it on a cereal packet. Stick this session's clue to the back of the packet.

⊕3 A surprise ending
⊕ *(10 minutes)*

What you need
- Bible, or copy of Luke 9:10–17 from page 16

What you do
Read out Luke 9:10–14 and ask the children what the problem was. When you have reviewed the situation, ask the children to work out some possible endings to the story. (Some children will know the story but encourage the entire group to think of different endings.) Then read them verses 15–17 to see what really happened. Talk about what sort of person Jesus was to do this.

⊕4 And the surprise was...
(15 minutes)

What you need
- Cards with the following statements on them: 'Over 5,000 people were hungry and they only had one packed lunch between them' (Luke 9:10–17).
  'A man was mugged and a priest, a Levite (priest's helper) and a man from Samaria came down the road' (Luke 10:29–37).
  'Jesus picked up a little child and spoke to the people' (Luke 9:46–48).
  'The blind man had been sitting by the roadside, begging, all his life' (Luke 18:35–43).
  'Zacchaeus the tax collector cheated people. No one liked him' (Luke 19:1–10).
- Five cards with, 'And the surprise was…' written on them
- Large sheets of paper or card
- Drawing materials

What you do
Read (or ask confident readers to read) each statement. Place a 'And the surprise was…' card by each statement and ask who can remember, from the DVD, what the surprise was. Divide the children into small groups, each with an adult helper. Each group chooses one of the statements, reads the Bible passage and makes a group poster to show the surprising ending. Share the posters afterwards and display them.

⊕5 On the news
(15 minutes)

What you need
- List of questions for each group (see page 23)
- A 'microphone' for each group

What you do
Read Luke 10:29–37 (the story of the good Samaritan). Divide the children into groups of five, if possible. One will be the mugged man/woman, one the priest, one the Levite, one the Samaritan and one the hotel manager. The adult team member in each group is the news reporter who interviews the people involved in this news story. Suggestions of questions are on page 23.

After all the questions have been asked, the interviewer can finish with:

'So, a surprising report all round. Something for us all to think about. If you have any information about the muggers, please contact *Landlubbers News*.'

Checklist
- Clue cards, today's clue (see page 19), glue sticks
- Shopping items and baskets to set the scene and maybe a poster 'Welcome to Landlubbers' Supermarket'
- *The Jesus Quest* DVD and television/ projector
- Next week's clue in cereal packet, written on the back of a cereal packet
- 'Landlubbers go to the supermarket' story (see page 45)
- Materials for your choice of activities for *Give us a clue*, *On the Jesus Quest* and *In the treasure chest*

⊞ ***When you see this logo, the activity is particularly appropriate for smaller groups.***

⊙⊙ ***When you see this logo, the activity will work well with older children.***

⊕ ***When you see this logo, the activity is key to the session.***

4

4

In the treasure chest

1 Landlubbers cafe
(10 minutes)

What you need
- A selection of different types of breads, crisps, cakes or cereals (it doesn't matter which – anything which reminds the children of the huge choice we have in our supermarkets)

What you do
Enjoy sharing the food together, maybe discussing choice and thinking about how amazing it is that we have such a range of good things to choose from. So often we take our packed supermarket shelves for granted. Develop the conversation further to explore what it is like to be hungry, and how the hungry crowd might have felt.

2 Bags of surprises
(15 minutes)

What you need
- Simple shopping bags with handles (enlarge the template on page 22), made of paper, card, felt or fabric
- Drawing and writing materials (or fabric pens/crayons/felt letters)
- Strips of paper with surprising things about Jesus written on them, eg
  'He fed 5,000 people with one packed lunch!'
  'He went to dinner with Zacchaeus!'
  'He told everyone they should be like children!'
  'He healed a man who had always been blind!'
  'He told a story with a surprising ending!'

What you do
Give out the shopping bags and ask the children to decorate their bag with the words, 'Jesus – full of surprises!' Fill the bag with the strips of paper with the surprising statements on. As you are working, talk about ways in which Jesus has surprised you (for more help on sharing your story with children, see page 12).

3 Supermarket quiz
(15 minutes)

What you need
- Empty food packets (mini cereal packets would be ideal)

- Questions on today's session, one stuck to each packet
- Pieces of paper with random numbers on, one placed in each packet

What you do
This is another opportunity for a quiz if you didn't use the one from last session, of if you'd like to do another! Make up a list of questions from the stories you have covered in this session. Divide the children into two teams. The teams take it in turn to choose a packet, answer the question on that packet, and then look inside to see what they've scored. When all the questions have been answered, the winning team is the one with the highest score.

4 QUESTion time
(10 minutes)

What you do
Check the treasure chest for new questions and answer them together. Remember to continue encouraging the children to put questions they would like to ask in the treasure chest. Make sure you include everyone in your discussions as you answer the questions.

5 Golden nugget verses
(10 minutes)

What you need
- Long strips of till roll (sold as calculator roll in stationery shops)
- Writing materials

What you do
If you haven't done an activity writing out Philippians 2:6,7 in previous sessions (or if you've concentrated on the first verse so far), give the children a length of till roll and writing materials so that they can write as much of the verses as they can each manage. As they do so, see if anyone can say the verses from memory. Encourage the children to take their till roll home and stick the verses somewhere prominent.

Extra for afterwards
Ask permission from your local supermarket and do some activities there (in small groups with adults), eg see how many fair-trade goods you can find; find something beginning with every letter of the alphabet.

Maybe you could offer to help pack people's shopping.

◑ Captains' story: Landlubbers go to the supermarket

'A visit to the supermarket is exactly what we need anyway,' said Captain Heave-ho, when they'd finished reading their next clue.

'Yeah, I'm getting a bit fed up with fish and chips for tea,' agreed Yo-ho, 'We need to get some supplies in. We'll go in the morning.'

'Do you think we should write a shopping list?' asked Yo-ho before they left for the local supermarket next morning.

'No,' said Heave-ho. 'We'll decide what we need when we get there. Mustn't forget peanuts for Nelson though!'

When the Landlubbers saw the supermarket, they were surprised by how big it was.

'It's ages since I've been shopping,' said Heave-ho. 'I got out of practice on the tropical island.'

'Me too,' whispered Yo-ho. 'It looks scary!'

'How can shopping be scary?' laughed Heave-ho, pulling out the biggest trolley he could find. 'Come on, I'll give you a ride!'

The pirates had a wonderful time taking turns in the trolley, with Nelson perched on the edge calling, 'Land ahoy! Land ahoy!' None of the other shoppers seemed to notice! Eventually though, after Yo-ho had taken a corner too quickly and upset a giant display of Alphabetti Spaghetti, they decided they ought to concentrate on buying something. They began in the breakfast aisle, and suddenly felt completely lost as at least thirty different types of cereal swam before their eyes. Ten minutes later they'd decided on Frostabix and Honey Puffs.

'We'd better get a move on,' said Heave-ho. 'We're going to be in here all day otherwise. Perhaps we should go in different directions!'

They did, and it was amazing how many adventures they both had! Yo-ho helped a lost boy to find his mum, after a store detective and a vicar walked straight past him!

'Who would have thought a pirate would have stopped to help!' said a checkout assistant to the boy's mother. Heave-ho helped an old woman do her shopping because everything she needed was on the top shelves and she was too short to reach. After about an hour their trolley was bulging. They wheeled it to the checkout.

'I hope we have enough gold!' said Yo-ho.

They did! When they got home, they were exhausted, so they sat down to munch Frostabix and watch the next episode of *The Jesus Quest*.

Show episode 4 of The Jesus Quest *DVD at this point. (Timings for* The Jesus Quest *video for this episode are 21.48 to 29.31.)*

'We had plenty of surprises in the supermarket,' said Yo-ho, excitedly, 'but I've had plenty more watching *The Jesus Quest* today.'

'Me too!' agreed Heave-ho. 'How did Jesus feed over 5,000 people with that little bit of food? And who would have thought Zacchaeus would change like that?'

'Who would have thought a Samaritan would have stopped to help that man,' added Yo-ho. 'Jesus is a surprising person to know.'

'And I'm glad we're getting to know him,' grinned Heave-ho. 'There's our next clue. Look! Written on the back of the packet of Frostabix.'

'A place with grass to run and play,
Its gates are open every day.
There are swings and a slide if you want a game, but
My favourite is the climbing frame!'

Tuned in – prayer activities

Choose one or both of these prayer ideas. *(10 minutes)*

Impossible prayers
What you do
Sit round in a circle and choose two really hard situations, where is it difficult to see how anything good could come out of it. Then speak to God about it, explaining afterwards to the children that we cannot always know what God will do (because he is a God of surprises) but we do believe he hears and is able to change

hard situations. Remember to come back to this next week.

If you are able to give a personal example of how God has surprised you by an answer to prayer, then do so now.

Till roll prayers
What you need
• Long strips of till roll (sold as calculator roll)
• Writing materials

What you do
Invite the children to write prayers on the till roll about

anything they'd like to say to God. Remind them that spelling doesn't matter to God – he will understand what they have written. Remind the children that God answers prayer in surprising ways. Use this opportunity to give an example. Prepare what you're going to say in advance.

You could close by reading Philippians 2:3

'Don't be jealous or proud, but be humble and consider others more important than yourselves.'

Landlubbers
go to the park

Aim **To find out how Jesus was welcomed as King when he arrived in Jerusalem.**
To begin to explore what kind of a king Jesus is and what that means for us.

Notes for you

When Jesus was welcomed into Jerusalem, there was a sense of celebration. There's a celebratory feel about today's activities too, but also an opportunity for the children to be quiet and thoughtful. Jesus was thoughtful as he looked beneath the celebrations and saw something in the temple which saddened him (the money changers) and something which gladdened him (the poor widow's offering). Pray that the children will begin to focus on King Jesus, who is fair and compassionate and who notices them.

The Jesus Quest episode covers: Jesus' entry into Jerusalem, the money changers in the temple, the widow's coin, the Last Supper and Judas' betrayal.

The key story is Jesus riding into Jerusalem.

Give us a clue

Welcome the children and give them their clue card and today's clue (about the park) to stick on to it. Help the children read the clue and remember where the Landlubbers will be going today. Then collect in the clue cards ready for next time. These activities introduce the park theme, the setting for the carnival in today's story, while in *The Jesus Quest*, Jerusalem is the setting for the Passover Festival.

⊜1 Make the sandwiches
(10 minutes)

What you need
- A table, a sliced loaf, butter or margarine, a pot of jam, a plate and knives for spreading for each team

What you do
Divide the children into teams and line them up at one end of your playing space. Set a table and sandwich-making ingredients opposite each team. The first person in each team runs to their table, puts two slices of bread on the plate and runs back to the back of their team. The next person butters the bread; the third person spreads jam on one of the buttered slices; the fourth person puts the two slices together and cuts them in half to make sandwiches. The fifth child starts the process again and so on. There should be an adult standing at each table to remind each child of their task and to supervise the cutting.

At the end of a given time, the team who has made the greatest number of sandwiches is the winner. You could also praise the neatest team, the most appetising sandwich or the jammiest sandwich!

⊜2 At the park
(15 minutes)

What you need
- A large playing space

Jesus – the king

- A selection of games equipment, eg plastic tennis rackets, balls of various sizes, hoops

What you do
Initiate a time of free play with the equipment. Join in where appropriate and encourage the children to interact positively and share the equipment. You may find in this activity that there are opportunities to talk to the children about the club. What do they enjoy the most? What do they think of Jesus so far?

⊜3 Design a mini-park
⊕ ☺ *(10 minutes)*

What you need
- Paper plates
- Plenty of mini-marshmallows and cocktail sticks (or art straws and pipe cleaners)

What you do
Set the materials out on tables and ask the children to design their own mini-park with swings, climbing frames and a football pitch (or whatever else they'd like to include). They should use the marshmallows to join the cocktail sticks together, to create the framework for their park. Enjoy looking at the end results together, praising each child for their efforts.

This activity was very popular at the Hothouse, especially as the marshmallows could be eaten afterwards!

On the Jesus Quest

⊕1 Landlubbers and Clues2Use
songs *(2 minutes)*

Sing the *Landlubbers* song and/or the *Clues2Use* song at this point, if you are using them.

 **Landlubbers go to the park**

(15 minutes)

What you need

- The Captains' story for session 5 (see page 49)
- *The Jesus Quest* DVD and TV/projector
- The clue for next session (see page 19), written on a piece of paper inside a lemonade bottle

What you do

Sit the children down so they can see both you and the television/screen. Remind everyone of this session's clue and read the Captains' story (Landlubbers go to the park). It leads straight into episode 5 of *The Jesus Quest* DVD. As you continue the story after the DVD, produce the next clue at the right time.

⊕3 What a welcome!

⊕ *(10 minutes)*

What you need

- Bible, or copy of Luke 19:28–38 from page 16

What you do

Divide the children into three groups, all sitting close together. Give each group one of these 'welcoming shouts':

Group 1 – 'Blessed is the king!'
Group 2 – 'Peace in heaven.'
Group 3 – 'Glory to God!'

Reassure the children that it doesn't matter if they can't remember it all – they're going to hear it as you read and they should repeat it after you. Also tell them that when they hear the word, 'Donkey,' all groups should say, 'Ee-aw.'

Read Luke 19:28–38, pausing where appropriate for the children to respond. Give everyone a time at the end of the reading where they can all shout their welcoming shouts together. Reflect for a moment on what this says to us about who Jesus is.

Afterwards, have a brief discussion about how we might welcome Jesus into our town. What might he choose to travel in/on? Why? Is this how we would expect a king or queen to arrive? What might we wave instead of palm branches? What would we shout?

⊕4 What Jesus saw!

(10 minutes)

What you need

- Bible
- Two large sheets of paper, one with an angry face in the centre and one with a smiley face
- Markers

What you do

Read Luke 19:45–48. Ask the children what it was that Jesus saw that made him so angry? (Some children may find it strange to think of Jesus being angry, so leave some space to discuss any questions they may have.)

Read Luke 21:1–4 about Jesus seeing the poor widow putting all she had into the temple offertory box. Ask the children what it was that Jesus saw that made him happy.

Place the two sheets of paper where everyone can see them and use them to record the children's thoughts as you discuss the following:

What do you think Jesus might see in our town/community that would make him angry?

What do you think Jesus might see in our town/community that would make him happy?

(If you have a large group, divide into smaller groups, with an adult in each group, so that each child has an opportunity to contribute.)

In the treasure chest

⊕1 Landlubbers cafe

(10 minutes)

What you need

- The sandwiches made earlier, if you did Give us a clue 'Make the sandwiches' (if you didn't, have some sandwiches ready for today's picnic-style refreshments)
- Anything else you might eat on a picnic, eg crisps, chocolate biscuits, mini-cheeses
- Paper tablecloths to spread out on the floor
- Paper plates

What you do

Enjoy sharing a mini-picnic together. Talk about what food a king or queen might eat at a banquet. Lead the discussion on to talk about what sort of a king Jesus was. What does it mean to you that Jesus is a king? How will you explain this to the children?

⊕2 QUESTion time

(10 minutes)

What you do

Check the treasure chest for new questions and answer them together. Remember to continue encouraging the children to put questions they would like to ask in the treasure chest. Make sure you include everyone in your discussions as you answer the questions.

Checklist

- Clue cards, today's clue (see page 19), glue sticks
- Play equipment – bats, balls, skipping ropes etc to set the scene
- *The Jesus Quest* DVD and television/projector
- 'Landlubbers go to the park' story (see page 49)
- Next session's clue written on a piece of paper and placed in an empty lemonade bottle
- Materials for your choice of activities for *Give us a clue*, *On the Jesus Quest* and *In the treasure chest*

 *When you see this logo, the activity is particularly appropriate for smaller groups.*

When you see this logo, the activity will work well with older children.

When you see this logo, the activity is key to the session.

⊙3 Celebration in the park
(at least 20 minutes)

The following activities create a carnival/festival atmosphere. Alongside them, the quiet area offers an opportunity for children who would like some space to think, especially about King Jesus.

What you need
- Equipment for simple 'stalls':
  Coconut shy – coconuts, sturdy plastic beakers, a table, juggling balls or beanbags
  Skittles – empty two-litre lemonade bottles with sand in them, tennis balls
  Guess where the treasure is – a simple treasure map divided into squares on which children can write their names
  Hoopla – rope cut up and taped to form rings, cans
  Carnival costumes – newspaper, crêpe and tissue paper, plastic offcuts, sticky tape, scissors
- 'Currency' (optional)
- Small prizes (optional)

What you do
Set up the stalls and activities around your room. (Your available space may or may not allow for all of the above.)

Invite the children to move around the stalls. Have an adult stallholder at each. If you are using 'currency' the children can 'pay' for their turn. Encourage them to use their 'money' wisely.

⊙4 Quiet corner
(all the session)

This could be available during each 'active' activity this session; at least during 'Celebration in the Park'

What you need
- A quiet corner of your room and low screens or chairs to define the area
- Rug and cushions
- Good quality Bible story books
- A CD player playing quiet worship music

What you do
Tell the children that the area is available, especially during the activity above, and that they don't have to spend all their time at the 'stalls'. If they do go to the quiet corner though, they are to use it well – to listen to music or look at books or to rest or talk to God.

After the activities, ask the children what they liked about having the quiet area. How would they have felt if people had come and behaved badly there? Remind them what they heard earlier about Jesus and the temple.

☞ *Our quiet area was visited and enjoyed by a few children we wouldn't have expected to go to it.* ☜

⊙5 Golden nugget verses
(10 minutes)

We have two new verses this session – Philippians 2:8,9. These will be the golden nugget verses for the rest of the series. These verses follow on from the verses we've used up to now and complete the picture of who Jesus is and what he did.

What you need
- Green paper cut in the shape of palm leaves, each with a word from Philippians 2:8,9 written on it (number the leaves so that the words can be easily sorted!)
- Drawing materials

What you do
Get the children to decorate the leaves and arrange them in the right order to say the verses. If you would like to encourage the children to learn the verses, try taking away a couple of leaves at a time, then saying the whole verse. How many can you take away before the children start to forget the verses?

Extra for afterwards
Have a group evening or day out to a really good park.

Do a 'litter pick' at your local park. (Remember that everyone should wear plastic gloves, and make sure the children are clear about what they should and should not touch.)

5

⊕ Captains' story: Landlubbers go to the park

'A trip to the park! I'll enjoy that!' said Captain Yo-ho, as they set off across town to find the nearest park. 'I hope there are swings. I miss sleeping in a hammock these days – the rocking of the swings will remind me what it was like. Maybe there will be a climbing frame too! I really miss climbing the rigging!'

'Climb the rigging! Climb the rigging!' called Nelson.

'It was a good idea of yours to bring a picnic,' said Heave-ho. 'A bit of fresh air is just what we need.'

As they got nearer the park, the Landlubbers realised that there were crowds of other people also making their way there.

'So much for peace and quiet,' said Heave-ho, 'There must be an event on.'

There was! It was the annual town carnival, and the captains watched with hundreds of others as the carnival floats arrived. As well as the floats, there were steel bands, dancers, ice cream vans and hot dog stalls. Many people were in fancy dress so Yo-ho and Heave-ho didn't feel out of place at all!

'Cool costumes!' said one girl, walking past.

'Realistic parrot,' said a boy as they waited in the queue for ice cream.

After a while, the carnival queen was crowned but there seemed to be a bit of a scuffle. As far as the Landlubbers could make out, the mother of the girl who came second in the Carnival Queen competition was saying that it wasn't fair. She said the winner's mother had paid extra money so that her daughter would win!

'I think we'll stay away from that argument,' said Yo-ho.'Sounds very dodgy!'

They managed to find a quiet spot to eat their picnic under the trees at the other end of the park, and then they had a great time on the swings and climbing frame. The trouble was, Yo-ho was over-enthusiastic, missed her footing and fell right from the top of the spider's web climbing frame.

'Ouch!' she said, holding her left arm.

'Time to go home and watch the next part of *The Jesus Quest*,' said Heave-ho, 'Don't worry, I'll carry the bag. Come on.'

Show episode 5 of The Jesus Quest *DVD at this point. (Timings for* The Jesus Quest *video for this episode are 29.31 to 36.51.)*

'That reminded me very much of our visit to the park today,' remarked Heave-ho afterwards.

'Yes,' agreed Yo-ho. 'But Jesus really was the king.'

'Not everyone recognised him, though,' said Heave-ho, 'and now he's been betrayed by one of his so-called friends. I don't believe it! Some people will do anything for money. It's dreadful! Is your arm OK now, Yo-ho?'

'No, it hurts like anything,' sighed Yo-ho. 'I'd better go to bed. We need the next clue first though.'

'It's here,' said Heave-ho, 'in an empty lemonade bottle left over from our picnic. It's ages since I had a message in a bottle!'

They read the clue together:
'People arriving with grapes and flowers,
Patients look forward to visiting hours.
Nurses, caring, smiling, smart,
Doctors checking someone's heart.'

Tuned in – prayer activities

Choose one or both of these prayer ideas. *(10 minutes)*

'Offering box' prayers

What you need
- A circular piece of gold card (large enough to write a prayer on) for each child
- Pens or pencils
- A box

What you do
Sit the children in a circle with the box in the centre and say that it's to remind us of the box the widow put her money in. Invite the children to write prayers on their 'coins' and put them in the box, just as the woman did, to show that they're giving them to God. Remind them that Jesus noticed the very small thing that the woman did. He notices the small things we do and he cares about them and us. Reassure any children who find it hard to write. One word or phrase, eg 'Thank you!', may be all that is needed.

Park prayers
What you do
Ask the children to think about their local park. What are the good things about it? What are the bad? Put the things the children have mentioned into a prayer.

You could close by reading Philippians 4:8:
'My friends, keep your minds on whatever is true, pure, right, holy, friendly and proper.'

Session 6

Luke
22:39–53

Aim To explore how Jesus might have felt when it seemed that all his friends were letting him down. To think about what it means for Jesus to be the friend who never ever lets us down. Because he loves us so much, he was prepared to go through with something very hard and he did it for us.

Notes for you

Many of the children will identify with what it feels like when a friend lets them down as, no doubt, you can. Give the group an opportunity to talk about this, and pray that the children will realise that, when they feel alone or scared, Jesus knows exactly how they feel and will always be there with them.

The Jesus Quest episode covers: the garden of Gethsemane, Peter's denial and Jesus' trial.

The key story is how Jesus is let down by Judas and Peter.

Landlubbers
go to the hospital

Give us a clue

Welcome the children and give them their clue card and today's clue (about the hospital) to stick on to it. Help the children read the clue and remember where the Landlubbers will be going today. Then collect in the clue cards ready for next time.

1 Jigsaw pieces
(10 minutes)

What you need

- Pictures (old calendar and greetings card pictures are good) cut up into five pieces (fewer if you have a young group)

What you do

Spread the picture pieces around your room, keeping back one piece from each picture. Ask the children to work in pairs or threes and give each pair a picture piece. Each pair looks for the rest of their pieces, puts their puzzle together and collects a new starter piece. The aim is to complete the most puzzles, and the theme reflects today's 'mending broken things' focus.

> *Our children loved this simple game, perhaps because it quickly gave them a sense of achievement.*

2 Bandage it!
(15 minutes)

What you need

- Bandages (alternatively make your own out of strips of material or use toilet rolls and sticky tape)
- A giant dice or enough small dice for each group to have one

What you do

Divide the children into groups and provide each group with bandages. Each group needs to select someone to be the 'casualty'. Then either:

- Have a leader in the centre of the room with the large dice and a list of which parts of the body will be bandaged when each number is thrown, eg 6: head, 5: body, 4: arm, 3: leg, 2: hand, 1: foot. The leader throws the dice, calls out which part of the body needs bandaging and the groups set to work, bandaging their casualties accordingly. The leader throws the dice again and so on until all the casualties are well bandaged!
- Give each group their own dice and list and let them throw their own numbers. Which team will be the first to finish?

Enjoy the results at the end of the game! Explain that being hurt and feeling pain is part of today's story.

3 Plaster of Paris
(10 minutes)

What you need

- Quick-setting Plaster of Paris (available in craft shops and some chemists)
- Moulds for plaster of Paris models.
- Water
- Spoons for mixing

What you do

Following the instructions on the packet, mix up the plaster with the children and help them to pour it carefully into the moulds. Then it needs to be left to set. Come back to the moulds at the end of the session when the children can enjoy taking the hardened plaster models out.

On the Jesus Quest

1 Landlubbers and Clues2Use songs *(2 minutes)*

Sing the *Landlubbers* song and/or the *Clues2Use* song at this point.

⊕2 Landlubbers go to the hospital
(15 minutes)

What you need

- The Captains' story for this session (see page 53)
- *The Jesus Quest* DVD and TV/projector
- The clue for next session (see page 19), written on a cardboard tube painted yellow

What you do

Sit the children down so they can see both you and the television/screen. Remind everyone of this session's clue and read the Captains' story (Landlubbers go to the hospital). It leads straight into episode 6 of *The Jesus Quest* DVD. As you continue the story after the DVD, produce the next clue at the right time.

> ⑤ *Sasha arrived at this session with a broken arm so she really identified with the story! Her plaster was red, not yellow like Captain Yo-ho's!* ⑤

⊕3 Night-time in the garden
⊕ *(10 minutes)*

What you need

- Bibles or copy of Luke 22:39–53 from page 17
- Torches or lanterns
- Enough sets of face cards for a set per child (see page 21)

What you do

Dim the lights (if you think your group will cope well with this) to give a night-time atmosphere. Have a few torches or lanterns to give some light. (If you're doing this session on a bright summer evening, don't worry!)

Give each of the children a set of face cards and ask them to imagine they are the disciples.

Read Luke 22:39–53 and ask the children to hold up their face cards at different points during the reading. They don't need to hold up the same card as their neighbour, just the card that depicts how they think they would be feeling at that point.

Afterwards, have a brief discussion about how Jesus was probably feeling, and why.

⊕4 Cock-a-doodle-doo!
(10 minutes)

What you need

- Bible

What you do

Sit the children in a circle and ask for a volunteer to be Peter, who then sits in the centre of the circle. Read Luke 22:54–62, inviting the children to repeat the words the bystanders say to Peter, with Peter repeating the replies, as they are read. When the cock crows, the children can give a rousing, 'Cock-a-doodle-doo!' Afterwards, have a brief discussion about how Peter was probably feeling, and why.

In the treasure chest

⊕1 Landlubbers cafe
(10 minutes)

What you need

- A choice of flavours of jelly (why not try fizzy jelly, made with lemonade?)
- Ice cream
- Bowls and spoons

What you do

Ask the children if they have been in hospital. Say that people used to have their tonsils out when they got sore. Explain what tonsils are. (It is rare for them to be removed now, so children may not have heard of them.) Ask the children to guess what kind of food people had to eat when they were recovering? Say that sometimes, people were given ice cream to eat. Serve the jelly and ice cream and enjoy talking as you all eat together.

⊕2 QUESTion time
(10 minutes)

What you do

Check the treasure chest for new questions and answer them together. Remember to continue encouraging the children to put questions they would like to ask in the treasure chest. Make sure you include everyone in your discussions as you answer the questions.

⊕3 Good friends
⊕ *(10 minutes)*

What you need

- Large sheets of paper (lining paper is ideal)
- Drawing and writing materials

Checklist

- Clue cards, this session's clue (see page 19), glue sticks
- Camp or fold-up bed, made up with a small table at the side with flowers and a bowl of grapes on it, to set the scene
- *The Jesus Quest* DVD and television/projector
- 'Landlubbers go to the hospital' story (see page 53)
- A cardboard tube, painted to look like a plaster cast, with next session's clue written on it
- Materials for your choice of activities for Give us a clue, On the Jesus Quest and In the treasure chest
- Letters inviting the children to come in their favourite football team's colours next session if they'd like to, if this is appropriate for your group

---

⊕ *When you see this logo, the activity is particularly appropriate for smaller groups.*

☺ *When you see this logo, the activity will work well with older children.*

⊕ *When you see this logo, the activity is key to the session.*

6

What you do

Divide the children into groups of not more than six. Choose someone in each group who is happy to lie down on the paper and be drawn around. Each group then fills this outline with the qualities they think a good friend should have. Do they know anyone who has all these qualities? What about Jesus? The children are all likely to have had experiences of friends letting them down. Give them an opportunity to share these. Share ways in which Jesus has been a good friend to you. It may be appropriate to challenge the children about what it means to become a friend of Jesus. If you need a structure to explain this, use the SU commitment booklets (see page 11) to guide your conversation.

4 Thinking of you
(15 minutes)

What you need
- Brightly coloured A4 card, folded in half
- Collage materials, glue and scissors
- Drawing/writing materials
- Envelopes

What you do

Ask the children to make either an 'I'm glad you're my friend' card, or a 'get well' card for someone they know. Get them to think about the kind of card their chosen person will really like and give them plenty of time so the cards can be special. Make envelopes available for the finished cards. This continues the 'being a good friend' theme. As you work, talk together about who the cards are for. Also take the opportunity to chat about what the children have learnt today.

5 Golden nugget verses
(at least 20 minutes)

What you need
- A large outline drawing of a bus
- Art materials

What you do

Write Philippians 2:8,9 on the side of the bus (where the adverts go) and divide your children into groups – a group to paint the bus, a group to draw or paint faces in the windows of the bus and a group to paint or draw Captain Yo-ho, Captain Heave-ho and Nelson the parrot waiting at the bus stop. Decide what you would like to do with this special picture. Maybe it could be placed in a prominent place in your church or hall. It will remind the children and may prompt people to pray for the club.

Extra for afterwards

Display the 'Bus Poster' your group has created.

Tuned in – prayer activities

Choose one or both of these prayer ideas. *(10 minutes)*

Grape prayers
What you need
- A bowl of seedless grapes

What you do

Sit the children in a circle and pass round the grapes. Ask each child to take a grape and think of a friend who they want to thank God for. They can say the name of the person out loud if they want to, and then eat the grape. Pass the grapes around again. This time, when they take a grape, ask the children to think of someone who is unwell or sad, or especially needs to know that Jesus is their friend and won't leave them. Again, invite them to say the person's name

and eat the grape. (Give the children an opportunity to say their own name if they want to.) If you have a large group, divide the children into smaller groups with a bowl of grapes for each, so no one has to wait too long for their turn.

'Garden of Gethsemane' prayer tree
What you need
- A large tree outline (with several branches) painted, drawn or stuck onto a dark background, or a few small branches secured in a pot of soil
- Leaf shapes of green paper (and string and sticky tape if you're using actual branches)
- Writing materials

What you do

Sit the children in a circle with the tree in the centre. Give a leaf shape to each child and ask them either to write a prayer, thanking Jesus for being such a good friend and never giving up; or to write their name, asking Jesus to help them to be a good friend. Stick the leaves on the tree, or, if you're using real branches, hang the leaves on the 'tree'.

Whichever prayer activity you choose, you may like to finish by reading Philippians 4:19:
'I pray that God will take care of all your needs with the wonderful blessings that come from Christ Jesus!'

⊕ Captains' story: Landlubbers go to the hospital

Captains Yo-ho and Heave-ho were waiting at the bus stop for the number 999 bus that would take them to the city hospital. Heave-ho was very excited.

'I'm really looking forward to going on a bus,' he chuckled. 'I wonder if it will be anything like being on board a ship again.'

'Shiver me timbers!' squawked Nelson, sharing Heave-ho's excitement.

'I shouldn't think it will be anything like being on board ship,' said Yo-ho, miserably. 'In fact, I hope it's not. I don't want my arm to be bumped about all over the place – it hurts enough as it is.'

'Oh, cheer up, Yo-ho! We're going to the hospital. It's a good thing that's where the next clue's taking us – they'll have your arm fixed in no time!'

'I don't want to go there,' muttered Yo-ho.

'Look!' shouted Heave-ho, ignoring her. 'Here comes the bus!'

'Land ahoy!' squawked Nelson.

They boarded the bus and, naturally, Heave-ho insisted they went upstairs. He even started singing sea shanties at the top of his voice, he was so excited; but Yo-ho just grew quieter and quieter.

When they eventually got off the bus, Yo-ho felt even worse. The hospital looked so big. Where would they go? What were they supposed to do here? She wished this wasn't part of the quest. Heave-ho was leading her through some automatic doors and before Yo-ho could say 'Pieces of eight' she was telling a friendly receptionist who she was and what had happened to her arm.

'Take a seat over there,' the receptionist said, 'You'll need to have it X-rayed to see whether you've broken a bone or not.'

The Landlubbers sat down in the crowded waiting room and were soon the centre of attention, as children came from various parts of the room to find out if they were real pirates and what the name of their parrot was.

'My son's completely forgotten his earache now he's met your parrot,' said a beaming mum.

Yo-ho wished she could forget her arm just as easily, but it hurt more than ever. They waited and waited. They waited so long that everyone lost interest in them and Heave-ho and Nelson fell asleep. Heave-ho was snoring loudly by the time Yo-ho went for her X-ray. She felt very alone. The doctor said she had broken her arm and would need to have it put in a plaster.

Soon, Yo-ho ran out of the plaster room, waving her fluorescent yellow arm in front of her.

'Look at this!' she said to Heave-ho, waking him up with her waving and shouting. 'I could even choose the colour!'

'A successful visit then,' said Heave-ho sleepily. 'Time to catch the bus home.'

'I think I might enjoy the ride myself this time,' smiled Yo-ho.

Show episode 6 of The Jesus Quest *DVD at this point. (Timings for* The Jesus Quest *video for this episode are 36.51 to 42.58.)*

'Do you know?' said Yo-ho, when she and Heave-ho had watched the next episode of *The Jesus Quest* that evening. 'Jesus knew just how I felt today, didn't he? He was scared and lonely in that garden, but he didn't give up. I'm sure he was there in the hospital with me today.'

'Yes,' agreed Heave-ho, thoughtfully. 'He's a good friend. He won't let anyone down, even though he was let down so badly himself. Now, where's the next clue?'

Yo-ho had a big grin on her face. 'You usually find it, Heave-ho, but today I have it. Look!'

And sure enough, there was a message written on her fluorescent plaster!

'Flags and scarves, a cheer, a shout!
Now the teams are coming out.
Free kick! Corner! Mexican wave.
Will it go in? Wow! What a save!'

Aim **To think about what happened when Jesus died on the cross and explore what it means to say that Jesus is our Saviour.**

Landlubbers
go to a football match

Notes for you

As you prepare this session, take time to reflect afresh on what Jesus dying on the cross means to you. The scenes of the crucifixion on *The Jesus Quest* DVD are moving. Give your children time to ask questions today if they need to. Pray that the children will be able to see beyond their fascination with the details, such as Jesus being nailed to the cross (important though these are), to why Jesus went through with it – so that each one of us can be forgiven for all that has prevented us from being God's friends and so that we may know how much he loves and cares for us.

The Jesus Quest episode includes: the carrying of the cross, the crucifixion and taking Jesus' body to the tomb.

 The key story is Jesus' death.

Give us a clue

Welcome the children and give them their clue card and today's clue (about going to a football match) to stick on to it. Help the children read the clue and remember where the Landlubbers will be going today. Then collect in the clue cards ready for next time.

1 Football team games
(10 minutes)

What you need
- A foam football for each team
- Cones or chairs

What you do
Line up the children in teams with a foam football for each team. Devise various team games using the football. They could be old favourites like 'tunnel ball' (sending the ball from the front to the back of the team through the tunnel of people's legs, the person at the end bringing the ball to the front and so on), and 'over and under' (one person passing the ball over their head to the person behind them, the next person passing the ball between their legs and so on), or a game in which each team member 'dribbles' the ball to the end of the playing space and back to their team. A row of cones or chairs could be placed in a row in front of each team for the players to go around.

2 Giant ball games
(10 minutes)

What you need
- A giant inflatable ball

What you do
Divide the children into two teams and number each child. Sit the teams either side of the playing space, with the ball in the centre. Call out a number. The two players with that number go to the ball and try to get it to their end of the playing space to score a goal.

Devise other games with the giant ball. Be particularly aware of younger children if you play any games involving your whole group at once.

Jesus – saviour

3 Human table football
(10 minutes)

What you need
- A foam football
- Chairs or cones

What you do
Divide the children into two equal teams. Decide who will be the two goalies and stand them at either end of your playing space with a goal (marked by two chairs or cones) behind them. The rest of the team members then line up in rows facing their goalie, making alternate rows with the opposing team. Each person links arms with the others in their row. Just like in table football, each row can move sideways but not forwards or backwards! They must stay linked – if the football lands near a player, they kick it.

On the Jesus Quest

1 Landlubbers and Clues2Use songs *(2 minutes)*

Sing the *Landlubbers* song and/or the *Clues2Use* song at this point, if you're using them.

2 Landlubbers go to a football match *(15 minutes)*

What you need
- The Captains' story for this session (see page 57)
- *The Jesus Quest* DVD and TV/projector
- The clue for next session (see page 19), written on a piece of paper and placed in an envelope

What you do

Sit the children down so they can see both you and the television/screen. Remind everyone of this session's clue and read the Captains' story (Landlubbers go to a football match). It leads straight into episode 7 of *The Jesus Quest* DVD. As you continue the story after the DVD, produce the next clue at the right time.

 What a save! 1
(10 minutes)

What you need

- A copy of Luke 23:26,27,32–49 for each reader, with their part underlined (see page 17)
- Hammer, nails and wood
- Dice
- A piece of material which can be ripped in half

What you do

Allocate the parts to confident readers or leaders (you will need people to read Jesus, Jewish leaders, soldiers 1 and 2, and criminals 1 and 2). Out of sight, but within earshot, station a leader with a hammer and nails and a piece of wood, and also a piece of material, which they can rip in half for the sound of the temple curtain. Station someone by the main lights so they can turn them (or some of them) off when the sky goes dark at 'midday'.

Read the passage slowly, with the sound and other effects at the appropriate points, and the allocated people reading the different voices. Ask the children for their comments and questions after the reading.

What a save! 2
(5 minutes)

What you need

- A picture of a football goal
- A picture of a goalie, a football and a cross (all with Blu-Tack on the back)

What you do

Start with the goalie stuck on to the picture in front of the goal net. Ask the children how they would feel if the goalie ran away as soon as they saw the football coming. Remove the goalie and stick a card football in the net. We can only say, 'What a save!' if the goalie stays and does their work. Remove the football and stick the cross in front of the goal net. Explain that Jesus stayed on the cross to save us from everything that was stopping us from being God's friends. He didn't run away. That's why we can say, 'What a save!' and call Jesus our 'Saviour'. Follow this up with *In the treasure chest* 'Odd balls'.

In the treasure chest

As you do these activities, talk about what it means to you that Jesus has saved you – saved you from being alone or feeling bad about the rotten things you have done, and saved you to live in a way that pleases him by not lying and so on. Think how you might explain this in a child-friendly way.

Landlubbers cafe
(10 minutes)

What you need

- Ring doughnuts

What you do

Serve the doughnuts to the children, explaining that they look a bit like lifebelts, which are used to save people in trouble in water. Enjoy eating the doughnuts and chatting together.

QUESTion time
(10 minutes)

What you do

Check the treasure chest for new questions and answer them together. Remember to continue encouraging the children to put questions they would like to ask in the treasure chest. Make sure you include everyone in your discussions as you answer the questions.

Football scarves
(15 minutes)

What you need

- Lengths of felt or paper in your local football team colours, cut into scarf shapes
- Smaller rectangles of felt or paper, their length being the same as the width of the long strips
- Felt or paper letters cut out to spell 'J E S U S'
- Fabric glue or glue sticks

What you do

Show the children the strips of felt or paper and ask them to make a football scarf for the local team. Stick the smaller rectangles at intervals along the long strip to make stripes. Then stick the letters J E S U S to the scarf.

Checklist

- Clue cards , today's clue (see page 19), glue sticks
- Blow up (or mini) football goal and football to set the scene
- Next session's clue in an envelope
- *The Jesus Quest* DVD and television/ projector
- 'Landlubbers go to a football match' story
- Materials for your choice of activities for *Give us a clue*, *On the Jesus Quest* and *In the treasure chest*

When you see this logo, the activity is particularly appropriate for smaller groups.

When you see this logo, the activity will work well with older children.

When you see this logo, the activity is key to the session.

7

 The Hothouse children loved making their scarves. We used felt (lots of claret and blue was needed because of where we live!) Sadly, our glue was rather runny and didn't stick very well so if you're using felt make sure you have fabric glue – it will make all the difference!

H4 'Jesus' chants
(10 minutes)

What you need
- Paper and pens or pencils

What you do
Divide the children into small groups and ask them to work out a football-style chant that says how great Jesus is, eg J E S U S! Jesus really is the BEST! Share the chants together afterwards.

H5 Odd balls
(10 minutes)

Use after *On the Jesus Quest* 'What a save! 2'.
What you need
- A picture of a football goal with a cross in front of it for each group
- Circular pieces of paper
- Writing materials and glue

What you do
Divide the children into groups, each with an adult leader. Give each group their picture, paper circles (footballs) and writing materials. Discuss with the children the types of thing Jesus was 'kicking out' when he died on the cross. Say that we sometimes call it sin. Write one suggestion on each ball (eg lying, being selfish, fighting) and stick the balls around the cross.

H6 Golden nugget verses
(10 minutes)

What you need
- A long piece of paper (lining paper is ideal)
- Paper of different colours and sizes, including newspaper
- Paint and glue

What you do
Follow the diagrams to tear a sheet of paper to make a cross. Stick the crosses all over the background and then ask for volunteers to paint one word each from Philippians 2:8 on top of the background: 'Christ was humble. He obeyed God and even died on a cross.' (Next session's golden nugget verse will complement this picture.)

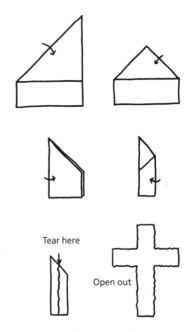

Tear here

Open out

Extra for afterwards
Maybe you could arrange a football session for those who are interested, or arrange to watch the next 'Big Match' together.

Tuned in – prayer activities

Choose one or both of the ideas here and opposite. *(10 minutes)*

Cross and nails prayers
What you need
- A cross made of two wooden batons, or a log of wood
- Hammer and nails
- Paper and writing materials

What you do
Sit the children in a circle with the cross or log in the centre. Give each child a piece of paper and invite them to write a 'sorry' prayer on it. (For some it will be enough just to write the word 'sorry'.) Invite the children to nail their prayers to the cross/log (supervising the nailing very carefully!) If you are not sure that your children will cope with this, or they are a young group, do the nailing yourself. The children are likely to be in a fairly serious mood and will therefore take this activity seriously. Pray that it will be so!

⊕ ■ Captains' story: Landlubbers go to a football match

'So our home team is [the local team] and our team colours are [the team's colours],' said Captain Yo-ho, checking that she had got it right. She and Heave-ho were queuing up for tickets for the football match.

'Yep, that's right,' replied Heave-ho, winding his newly bought supporters' scarf around his neck. Several minutes later, they had made their way to the East Stand. The stadium was packed, thousands of fans were already singing and chanting loudly. Nelson, for once, was very quiet indeed and snuggled himself down inside Heave-ho's jacket for some peace! All around them, [Insert the local team's colours] scarves and flags were waving. In the West Stand at the other end of the pitch they could see the orange and grey scarves and flags of the away team supporters.

'This is going to be a little different from football as we know it,' commented Heave-ho. 'A pitch marked out on the sand and a coconut for a ball is more what we're used to.'

'Yeah,' agreed Yo-ho, 'and I never did like it much. Those coconuts really bruised your toes if you kicked them hard.'

'And the ball was almost always stolen by monkeys before the match was over!' added Heave-ho, laughing. 'Look! Here come the teams. The game's about to start!'

The Landlubbers were soon engrossed in the match. When their team scored twice in the first half they went wild with excitement, just like the rest of the home fans.

'Two-nil! Two-nil! Two-nil!' they sang.

'Shiver me timbers!' squawked Nelson from inside Heave-ho's jacket. At half-time, Heave-ho offered to go and buy refreshments.

'You stay here, Yo-ho,' he said. 'You don't want to get your arm bashed in the crush.'

So Yo-ho stayed where she was while Heave-ho went and bought doughnuts. Somehow, Heave-ho managed to get himself lost. At the beginning of the second half, he was very surprised to find himself in the West Stand, surrounded by orange and grey. What's more, the away team quickly scored. All around him people cheered and sang. It didn't feel right at all and as soon as he could, he made his way back to the East Stand where the home supporters were shouting. 'What a save! What a save! What a save!' as their goalie stopped an equaliser. Ten minutes later though, the score was two-all. Then things went from bad to worse when the away team scored the winning goal, a minute before the final whistle.

'How disappointing,' sighed Yo-ho. 'I was sure we were going to win.'

'Me too,' agreed Heave-ho. 'Just shows how wrong you can be. Come on, let's go home and watch *The Jesus Quest*.'

Show episode 7 of The Jesus Quest *DVD at this point. (Timings for* The Jesus Quest *video for this episode are 42.58 to 49.56.)*

For a few minutes after watching episode 7 of *The Jesus Quest* neither of the captains spoke. Then, Heave-ho said quietly, 'Now I know why the Quest took us to the football match.'

'Do you?' said Yo-ho, sounding surprised.

'Yes,' said Heave-ho slowly. 'When I got lost at half-time, I ended up with the supporters of the other side. When Jesus was crucified, he ended up with the supporters of the other side.'

'I suppose he did,' said Yo-ho, 'and his own supporters were so disappointed because they thought they'd lost.'

'But they hadn't, had they?' said Heave-ho. Things began to click into place! 'What they should have been shouting was, 'What a save! What a save! What a save! Only it didn't seem like it at the time.'

Suddenly, an envelope came flying through their rusty letterbox – the final clue!

'Landlubbers, here's your invitation,
You're welcome at the celebration.
You've looked north and south, east and west.
Today you'll complete the Jesus Quest!'

Tuned in – prayer activities

'Magic' slate prayers

This prayer activity was also suggested in Session 3, but if you didn't use it then it is also relevant for this session. Or if it went especially well, you could use it again.

What you need

• 'Magic slates' (one per pair)

What you do

Invite the children to take it in turns, in their pairs, to write a 'sorry' prayer, and then watch as their partner rubs it out. Say that this is what happened when Jesus died on the cross. He forgives us for all the things that have stopped us being friends with God.

End with Philippians 3:14:
'I run towards the goal, so that I can win the prize of being called to heaven. This is the prize that God offers because of what Christ Jesus has done.'
(This is the key verse in session 4 of the *Landlubbers* holiday club programme.)

Luke
24:1–10 (and 24:36–43)

Aim **To celebrate the fact that Jesus came alive again. This means that he is exactly who he says he is, and is able to give us new life with him forever.**

Landlubbers
go to a party

Jesus – the Son of God

Give us a clue

Welcome the children and give them their clue card and today's clue (about the party) to stick on to it. Help the children read the clue and remember where the Landlubbers will be going today. Then collect in the clue cards but remember to give them out at the end of the session for the children to take home.

Notes for you

Jesus went to a lot of trouble to ensure that his disciples were absolutely sure he was alive again! God sent angels to the tomb to remind them that Jesus said he would rise again; Jesus talked with his disciples, together and individually. He showed them his hands, feet and sides. He ate with them. He wanted them left in no doubt. Pray that the children in your group will be left in no doubt that Jesus is alive and that some of them may be ready to explore further how he can make a difference to their lives.

The Jesus Quest episode includes: the women at the empty tomb, Jesus appearing to the disciples.

 The key story is Jesus meeting the women at the tomb.

1 Favourite games
 (15 minutes)

What you need
- Any equipment you need to play the favourite games from earlier sessions, or games you played at the *Landlubbers* holiday club, if you had one.

What you do
Set up the games and enjoy playing them!

⊖2 **Piñata**
(10 minutes)

This is a lot of fun and creates a party atmosphere. It can also set the scene for thinking about the resurrection of Jesus. Suddenly the sweets come bursting out of the piñata. Suddenly the risen Jesus burst out of the cold, dark tomb.

What you need
- A bought or home-made Piñata (originally from Mexico, piñatas are full of sweets or small gifts)
- Several rolled-up newspapers

What you do
A home-made piñata can either be made from papier mâché (using a balloon as a base) or from two hanging basket inners (the pulpy card type). Fill with the sweets or gifts and then securely tape the two halves together. Tape a string securely round the piñata leaving an end free for hanging it up. Cover the piñata with brightly coloured wrapping paper.

Stand the children in a circle. Ask someone tall to stand in the centre holding the piñata by its string, or hang from the ceiling. Let the children take it in turns to hit the piñata with the rolled-up newspapers. Eventually the piñata will burst open and everyone can share the sweets and gifts. An added excitement is to blindfold the children before they beat the piñata.

⊖3 **Biscuit icing**
(10 minutes)

What you need
- Biscuits (either bought rich tea type biscuits or home-made biscuits – butterfly-shaped would be good as a sign of new life)
- Icing in all colours of the rainbow
- Sprinkles, thin licorice laces, other decorations
- Teaspoons and blunt knives for spreading

What you do
Give the children biscuits to ice and say that you will be sharing them later at the Landlubbers cafe. Have fun icing the biscuits and chatting about how the children are decorating theirs.

On the Jesus Quest

⊕1 **Landlubbers and Clues2Use songs** *(2 minutes)*

Sing the *Landlubbers* and/or the *Clues2Use* song at this point, if you are using them.

⊕2 **Landlubbers go to a party**
(15 minutes)

What you need
- The Captains' story for this session (see page 61)
- *The Jesus Quest* DVD and TV/projector

What you do

Sit the children down so they can see both you and the television/screen. Remind everyone of this session's clue and read the Captains' story (Landlubbers go to a party). It leads straight into episode 8 of *The Jesus Quest* DVD.

3 Really Alive! 1
(10 minutes)

If at all possible find time for both Bible passages, as they are both key. If half the group looks at one and half at the other, a much better overall picture is gained. Do make sure you share what it means to you that Jesus is alive.

What you need

- Bibles or copies of Luke 24:1–10 from page 18
- Magnifying glasses (there are usually sets available at 'pound' shops)
- Card cut out in the shape of a magnifying glass
- Writing materials

What you do

Read Luke 24:1–10 about the women going to the tomb. The problem to be solved is: How did the women know that Jesus was really alive again? Tell the children that we're going to be like detectives and look very carefully at the passage for clues. Give out magnifying glasses and copies of the passage to pairs of children. (Make sure less confident readers are with someone who can support them.) Also, have card magnifying glasses ready to write on. Ask the children to give you their evidence from the passage. This can then be written on the card magnifying glasses, eg the stone was rolled away; the body wasn't there; the angels gave a message; Jesus said he would rise again.

4 Really Alive! 2
(10 minutes)

Use Luke 24:36–43 instead of, or as well as, the one above. You could divide your group into two, get the groups to report back and put all the evidence together.

What you need

- The same resources as for 'Really Alive!' 1
- Bibles or copies of Luke 24:36–43 from page 18

What you do

Use the same method as for 'Really Alive' 1. This time, the problem to be solved is: How did Jesus' disciples know Jesus was really alive?

The evidence this time could be: Jesus appeared and talked to his disciples; Jesus invited them to touch him; Jesus showed them his hands and feet; Jesus asked for food; Jesus ate food.

After hearing the 'evidence' from both passages, ask the children, 'How does this make us feel?' 'What difference does it make?' Give them an opportunity to share their thoughts and ask questions. Sum up by saying it shows that Jesus really is who he says he is; that all the things we've been finding out about him over the sessions are true, and that he can make a difference to us now, all through our lives and beyond.

> *Our children enjoyed using the magnifying glasses. Several of them wanted to read the verses to the rest of the group and they were quick to find the evidence. A mum who chose to stay for the session also joined in.*

5 Challenge
(10 minutes)

You may have been able to explain clearly over the last few weeks what it means to be a friend of Jesus and be sure that the children have each made an appropriate response, depending on where they are in their spiritual journey. However, you may think that some children still need to be challenged to make a further commitment to Jesus. If so, show the final part of *The Jesus Quest* DVD, which gives the children a challenge. Be prepared to talk with them individually afterwards.

In the treasure chest

Use this time to talk together about what you have enjoyed and discovered during *Clues2Use*.

1 Landlubbers cafe
(10 minutes)

What you need

- Rainbow-coloured food and drink (including the iced biscuits from earlier, if you made them)
- Party music

What you do

This is a real party today, so try and emphasise the party atmosphere as you share the party food together. Do all you can to make this as enjoyable as possible.

Checklist

- Clue cards, today's clue (see page 19), glue sticks
- Balloons, bubble machine and party decorations to set the scene
- *The Jesus Quest* DVD and television/ projector
- 'Landlubbers go to a party' story (see page 61)
- Materials for your choice of activities for Give us a clue, On the Jesus Quest, and In the treasure chest

When you see this logo, the activity is particularly appropriate for smaller groups.

When you see this logo, the activity will work well with older children.

When you see this logo, the activity is key to the session.

8

⊕2 QUESTion time
(10 minutes)

What you need
- The QUESTion time treasure chest
- Some commitment booklets of the appropriate age (see page 11)
- Pieces of pirate-shaped paper (see page 22)
- Pencils

What you do
Use the chest as a place where children can post their own responses to Jesus and what they've found out about him during this series. Give them some space and time to do this and to talk to the leaders if they want to. Show them the booklets and say that if anyone would like one they can ask you at the end of the session.

⊕3 Celebration gardens
(10 minutes)

What you need
- Small seed trays
- Sterile compost, moss, pebbles, flowers, twigs, grass seed, other materials to create a garden
- Shallow containers (for ponds)
- Small pulp flowerpots (for the cave)

What you do
Give each child a seed tray and show the materials you have brought with you. Ask them to create a garden with what they have, making sure they create a cave with a flowerpot, complete with a pebble which can be rolled away. Help any children as necessary, and chat about today's story. What do the children think about what they have heard today? When you have finished, admire the gardens, making sure you compliment every one.

⊕4 Butterfly badges
(15 minutes)

What you need
- Butterfly shapes cut out of card (see page 22)
- Collage materials
- Art materials
- Safety pins
- Sticky tape and glue

What you do
Ask the children to decorate a really special butterfly badge to remind them of the new life Jesus gives. Tape a safety pin to the back and let the children decide whether to keep or give away their butterfly.

⊕5 Golden nugget verses
(10 minutes)

What you need
- A long piece of paper (lining paper is ideal)
- Brightly coloured and metallic paper
- Pencils, scissors and glue
- Paint

What you do
Ask the children to draw and cut out paper crown shapes. (Some children will need help in drawing a crown, but there will be much more variety if as many as possible can design their own.) Stick the crowns all over the lining paper, and then ask for volunteers to write out (with paint) one word each of Philippians 2:9 on top of the background of crowns: 'Then God gave Christ the highest place and honoured his name above all others.'

This poster can be displayed with last session's golden nugget verse.

Extra for afterwards

Maybe you could invite everyone to church for a special celebration service, especially if you finish this series near Christmas or Easter. Maybe, if you have children in your group who have never been inside your church, you could arrange a visit for them and show them around. Make sure that children and parents and carers know about what else is going to happen in future weeks in the club, church or community.

Don't forget, you may want to offer each child their own copy of *The Jesus Quest* DVD. For details of where to order these, see page 62.

When the children have gone, spend time praying together for the Holy Spirit to continue to be active in the lives of the children and their families. Thank God for all the things that have happened over the last eight sessions. How will you follow up what has already begun? See page 13 for more ideas.

⊕ █ Captains' story: Landlubbers go to a party

'An invitation!' shouted Heave-ho. 'Just what we need – a good party!'

'It doesn't say where it is though,' said Yo-ho thoughtfully, 'or even who it's from. I didn't think we knew anyone here well enough to be invited to a party.'

'That's true,' admitted Heave-ho, polishing up his shoe buckles. 'The clues have always told us where to go before, haven't they? Still, it's bound to become obvious. Come on, Yo-ho. Shine up your boots. We can't ignore this!'

Ten minutes later, Captains Yo-ho and Heave-ho were looking their smartest and Nelson's feathers were looking particularly glossy and fine. They opened their old front door to begin their search for the celebration.

'Maybe we'll have to go on another bus,' said Heave-ho. 'In fact, I think I'd like to have a go driving the bus next time!' Then he stopped in his tracks as an amazing sight met their eyes.

'We don't have to look for the party at all!' laughed Yo-ho. 'It's a party here in our street!'

Sure enough, the shabby little street had been transformed. There were balloons and streamers and banners of all colours of the rainbow, flying from every house. Right down the middle of the street there were tables covered with bright cloths, covered with everyone's favourite food. There were pizzas and garlic bread, burgers and hot dogs, chocolate-spread sandwiches and sausage rolls. There were salads and fruit, jelly and ice cream, cakes and chocolate biscuits, pickled onions and crisps. Up and down the road, arriving from all directions, there were people all waving their invitations. The Landlubbers recognised the homeless man they had seen when they first arrived; the children who had been playing football with the can; some of the people from the swimming lesson; the head

teacher and some children from the school; the lost boy and his mum whom Yo-ho had helped in the supermarket; the old woman Heave-ho had helped; the girl who had won second place in the Carnival Queen competition; the friendly receptionist and doctor from the hospital, as well as the boy with the earache; football players from both teams and the driver from the number 999 bus, as well as many others.

The captains sat themselves down between a boy who had been Batman at the carnival and a girl who had been selling popcorn at the cinema, and began to enjoy themselves. (Nelson was happy too, especially when he spied the dishes of peanuts and plates of fruit). The party lasted all day! Once it began to rain, but huge umbrellas appeared over every table. As it rained, the sun continued to shine and a magnificent rainbow appeared in the sky. At last, tired but happy, Yo-ho and Heave-ho made their way home. They still had something very special to do.

Show episode 8 of The Jesus Quest *DVD at this point. (Timings for* The Jesus Quest *video for this episode are 49.56 to 56.11.)*

'Wow!' said Heave-ho as *The Jesus Quest* DVD came to a close. 'What an ending! What a party!'

'It's not an ending really, is it?' remarked Yo-ho. 'It's more a beginning. Jesus the Son of God is with us for ever. We can be with him for ever.'

'Hmm,' said Heave-ho, nodding his head, 'That's what our celebration was all about today then. What I don't understand though, is why not everyone we'd met on the Jesus Quest was there. They must have all been invited.'

'Ahhh,' said Yo-ho, 'but for some reason not everyone answered their invitation.'

'Well, I'm glad we did,' replied Heave-ho.

'Me too! Me too! Me too!' squawked Nelson.

'Me too,' whispered Yo-ho. 'The others just don't know what they're missing.'

Tuned in – prayer activities

Choose one or both of these prayer ideas. *(10 minutes)*

Parachute praise
What you need
- A parachute

What you do
Stand everyone around the parachute, holding the edge. Invite everyone to think of something they would like to say 'thank you' to God for.

They then take it in turns. After each 'thank you', everyone lifts the parachute shouting, 'Lord, we lift our praise to you!'

Balloon praise
What you need
- An inflated balloon per child
- Markers to write on balloons

What you do
Give everyone a balloon and ask them to write 'Thank you,

God!' on it. Stand everyone in a circle and invite them to think of something they would like to say 'thank you' to God for. They take it in turns to do so. After each 'thank you', bat that child's balloon once around the circle.

You may like to end by reading Philippians 4:4

'Always be glad because of the Lord! I will say it again: be glad.'

About Agapé

Agapé is an evangelistic organisation working with people of influence in most areas of life – in communities, workplaces, schools and universities.

Three key words in the organisation are Win, Build and Send: **Win** people to Christ, **Build** them in their faith and **Send** them out to win, build and send others. This is reflected not just in the work the staff are engaged in, but also in the resources and training they offer to churches and Christian groups for local mission.

Agapé holds the distribution rights in UK to the JESUS film, which has now been translated into over 850 languages and has been seen by over 2 billion people. *The Jesus Quest* was produced to help a growing generation of children see the story of Jesus from the perspective of the young.

In the UK the organisation has over 100 full-time staff and is a member of the Evangelical Alliance and Global Connections

At its heart, Agapé is helping build spiritual movements everywhere so that everyone knows someone who truly follows Jesus

For more information contact:

Agapé, Fairgate House, Kings Road, Tyseley, Birmingham B11 2AA
Tel: 0121 765 4404, Fax: 0121 765 4065
Email: info@agape.org.uk, Web: www.agape.org.uk

To order resources:

Phone their Orderline: 0121 683 5090 or email sales@agape.org.uk

The Jesus Quest is available on DVD from September 2005, £3.99 each or £75 for a box of 25. A small postage and packing charge will be added to all orders.

The schools' edition of *The Jesus Quest* is available on DVD, costs £25.00 (plus p&p) and comes with a CD containing lesson plans, children's activities and help for teachers.

After Clues2Use

Have you tried...

Streetwise

Julie Sharp and Claire Derry

Get streetwise and pop into eight homes that Jesus visited – the cheat's house, the crowded house, the rich man's house – all houses that feature in Luke's Gospel. Another eight-session programme from Scripture Union, aimed at groups that attract children with no church connection. (This programme also works with the *Luke Street* video.)

Resource book: £8.99, 1 85999 767 8

DVD: £14.99, 1 84427 111 0

Books
to help you

Jesus and the starving crowd
Diane Walker

The story of Jesus feeding more than 5,000 people is beautifully retold in *Jesus and the starving crowd*. It is available in two formats, a big book for group use and a child's reader.

Big Book: £19.99, 1 85999 722 8

Child's reader: £3.50, 1 85999 723 6

Others in the series include:

Jesus and the cheat, Jesus puts things right and *Jesus and the breakfast barbecue*

Kids' Culture
Nick Harding

Discover the key issues children face today - at home, school, through TV, music and books - and help them find the good and God in their world.

£8.99, 1 85999 676 0

To order these or any of Scripture Union's products, visit your local Christian bookshop or contact SU Mail Order:

Scripture Union Mail Order, PO Box 5148, Milton Keynes MLO, MK2 2YX

Tel: 0845 07 06 006 Fax: 01908 856020 Web: www.scriptureunion.org.uk *Prices correct at time of going to press.*

After Clues2Use

Have you tried...

Awesome!
Sue Clutterham

Jesus can do amazing things – awesome! Discover the signs in John's Gospel to find out who Jesus is, while watching the Awesome! DVD and having a fantastic time! Another eight-session programme from Scripture Union, aimed at groups that attract children with no church connection. (This programme also works with the *Signposts* video.)

Resource book: £8.99, 1 84427 153 6

DVD: £14.99, 1 84427 159 5

eye level clubs...

- are for boys and girls aged 5 to 11.
- are for children who are not yet part of a church (as well as those who are).
- don't assume that children know much about Jesus or have had any experience of church.
- recognise that all children are open to God and the wonder of his world, and that all children can have valid spiritual experiences, regardless of church background.
- aim to give children one of the best hours in their week.
- provide opportunities for appropriate and respectful relationships between children and adults, working in small groups.
- plan to introduce children to the Bible in ways that allow for imagination, exploration and learning difficulties.
- are led by those who long to see children become lifelong followers of Jesus Christ.
- are led by those who will put themselves at a child's level, so that together they can catch sight of Jesus.